W9-DDI-013

CONSULTATIVE SELLING

Consultative Selling

REVISED EDITION

MACK HANAN

JAMES CRIBBIN

HERMAN HEISER

amacom

A DIVISION OF AMERICAN MANAGEMENT ASSOCIATIONS

© 1973 AMACOM

A division of American Management Associations,
New York. All rights reserved. Printed in the United
States of America.

International standard book number: 0-8144-5328-7
Library of Congress catalog card number: 73-75769

Eleventh Printing

PREFACE

SUCCESSFUL COMPANIES come in many styles and sizes. Nearly every industry has one or two. In our role as consultants, we have a unique opportunity to seek out the common denominators among them: the small number of characteristics that we can say accompany success even if we cannot always prove they have caused it. One discovery we have made over and over again is that successful companies concentrate their sales function on a relatively small number of key accounts.

By calling attention to key-account concentration, we are not ignoring the care and feeding of new, young growth accounts. Nor are we denying the contribution that small or occasional customers can make to paying for overhead, achieving budgets, and adding the marginal profits that often make the difference between a good year and a great year. What we are centering on is the bull's-eye position which key accounts generally hold for successful companies. These are the accounts they plan around. These are the accounts they serve with their most abundant resources and their most professional salesmen. These are in effect the heart of their business, and they renew their dedication to these key customers again and again every morning when they open their doors.

From the key-account salesman's point of view, as well as those of the regional, district, and general headquarters where his managers sit, serving a major customer is the most difficult task in selling. So much rides on it. Almost every key account has a long history of painstaking development behind it. Yet it can all be blown in an instant. Once lost, key accounts are exceedingly difficult to recapture or replace. Their sales are almost impossible to make up quickly. Even if the same volume can be gained back from other customers, the replacement sales may be nowhere near as profitable as those from the lost account.

"Hold on to your key accounts" is the watchword of every successful business. Key accounts are not only the best customers; they are also the best prospects for added business. But how can key accounts be won? Once won, how can they be maintained?

In the 1960s the three of us set out to find answers to these questions. For many years we have helped recruit key-account salesmen, train and develop them, and counsel them. Now we decided to analyze them to see what it was they were doing that worked well for them, what services they were providing, what needs they were fulfilling, what plans they were making to create successful new customer relationships or perpetuate existing ones.

Time and again in the course of our study, we gained a fascinating insight. So many of the things a good key-account salesman was doing with his major customers were practically identical to many of the strategies that we ourselves, as consultants, regularly apply to our own clients. And sure enough, when we made the salesmen and their accounts aware of our insight, many of them told us that they had come to recognize this parallel for themselves as their relationships matured. By way of confirmation, one salesman showed us a business card which he had had created at his own expense. Underneath his name was a new title he had given himself: *account consultant*. The title made it easier for him to operate consultatively, he said. But he and all the other key-account salesmen we analyzed told us that working in this way is a tough way to do business. Nobody teaches it. Every man has had to learn it for himself. Trial and error seems to be the only method available. "You're always on trial and the errors can kill you."

We determined that, instead of standing idly by while every generation of key-account salesmen learned *consultative selling* for themselves, we would try to organize it, clarify it, and teach it as a formal discipline.

We approach consultative selling on the premise that the salesman's role with a key account is a multidisciplined one which combines three major strategies. First is a group of customer relations strategies which together enable the salesman to relate closely and confidentially to his key accounts over a long period of time. This discipline is the province of Dr. James Cribbin, a management psychologist. The second strategy that is part of consultative selling is the ability of a salesman to embed his products and services into the long-term business plans of his key accounts. This discipline is the province of Mack Hanan, a planner of business growth strategies. The third strategy focuses consultative selling squarely on the target of profit improvement, both for the salesman's management of his own business and for his ability to plan the profit improvement of his key accounts. This discipline is the province of Herman Heiser, a certified public accountant and profit planner.

We have consolidated our areas of experience into a unified approach that is centered on planned profit improvement for both the salesman and his key accounts. This approach rests on five foundations. One is for the salesman to build a climate of confidence into his customer relationships that will reposition his role to a consultative one. It will also enable him to convert his customers into clients. Unless this conversion takes place, no consultation can occur. A second foundation is the miniaturized business plan, which we call the miniplan. This puts the salesman's business with his accounts on a professionally planned basis. The third foundation is to use the plan's framework to negotiate mutual profit improvement projects as the main function of the consultative relationship. In the negotiation process, the two remaining foundations of our approach become evident. We recommend that systems of strategies be put together to serve the customer's objectives for profit improvement and the salesman's objectives for profitable sales. And we instill a strong control system into the plan's operations so that a true partnership can be achieved.

The intent of our approach is not to transform salesmen into consultants. A salesman does not have to become a psychologist in order to perceive the major characteristics of his key customers' personalities that influence their decision making. Nor will a salesman have to become an accountant in order to help his key accounts plan for profit improvement; he can learn to plan profit perceptively, without access to many financial facts and even without a mind for numbers. And he can learn to set forth profit improvement objectives and strategies in the form of a miniplan that makes it unnecessary for him to become a professional business planner.

Our three disciplines, we now say, belong in every key-account salesman's tool kit. They are the talent base he must operate from. Similarly, they are the curriculum he must be trained in if he is to be a genuinely professional practitioner. For the product salesman, time and territory management, precall planning and postcall follow-up, techniques of overcoming objections, and the strategies of closing have been the traditional catechism. Now, for the consultative salesman, we are prescribing the three basic strategies of customer relations management, business planning, and profit improvement.

On many occasions, we have more or less humorously questioned each other about which of our three disciplines is actually the most important one. Salesmen have asked us the same question—mostly, we suspected, in the hope that they could learn which disciplines it would be safest to short-sheet. At first we tended to resolve this prickly issue by relating it to the three-legged stool: Which one of *its* legs is the most important? The obvious answer, they *all* are, left us initially mollified but eventually curious again. Which one of us *were* the other two really working for?

Our answer, which took longer in coming than we would have liked and which surprised us when it did, now seems obvious. Dr. Cribbin's *climate of confidence* is the most important leg of the stool. Without it there can be no consultative relationship: no long-term planning of the salesman's business with a key account, no profit improvement objectives, nothing. So it turns out that instead of two of us possibly working for the third, Dr. Cribbin's discipline is really working for the other two. It is the ability of his approach to create the environment in which consultative selling must take place that gives our other two disciplines the legs they need to stand on.

We try to teach our three strategies in the same integrated manner in which the consultative salesman must apply them in the real world of customer service. He cannot say, "Now I am practicing a consultative type of customer relations by negotiating with my account's decision maker instead of trying to persuade him," and then at some later point, "Now I am planning to improve his profit." He will of course be doing these things simultaneously as he negotiates for profit improvement. As you read this book in which—owing to the requirements of publishing logic—we present our disciplines sequentially instead of simultaneously, we ask that you keep this difference in mind.

There is, as well, one more point worth remembering. In creating the consultative selling approach we have said to ourselves that it must offer *an alternative to selling on price* in the face of intense competition between standardized commodity products which offer neutralized benefits. If it cannot do this for a company, it can have no value. We have also set what we think of as ultimate criteria. There are two of them. One is that consultative selling must work for a company even when it is quite frankly the high-priced supplier in its field. Second, consultative selling must work even when the company is not the highest-quality supplier in its field. These two situations are the acid test for any sales strategy. They are no less so for the strategy of selling consultatively, and it is on the ability of our approach to help key-account salesmen meet these criteria that we rest our case.

In the mid-1960s, when we took the first steps to integrate our three diverse disciplines into the single system we call consultative selling, we became aware that our mission was going to be similar to the mission we were prescribing for key-account salesmen: We would have to install our system into a key process of our clients—in this case, their sales process—if we wanted it to work. We were fortunate in finding the few men of boldness we needed to help us put our system to the acid test. This revised edition of our book is just as much their book in many respects as it is our own. For this reason, we want to acknowledge our indebtedness to Ed Holder, John Foley, and Phil Smith of the Continental Can Company and to Joe Page and Chuck Crowe of

McGraw-Hill, all of whom have worked closely with us in the climate of confidence we advocate. At an even earlier date, Bob Hutchings of IBM provided a forum for some of our front-running ideas that later became important aspects of *Consultative Selling*. Finally, we want to thank Bob Albert and Marty Everett of *Sales Management* magazine for giving us the opportunity to receive industrywide reaction to our thinking by publishing many of our emerging ideas as we have generated them.

MACK HANAN
JAMES CRIBBIN
HERMAN HEISER

CONTENTS

1/The Consultative Selling Approach

ONE OF THE FEW universal facts of selling is the 80–20 rule. The rule says that somewhere up to 80 percent of almost every company's sales may come from fewer than 20 percent of its customers. Every business rests on this kind of relatively small foundation of heavy, repeat customers who are its key accounts. These are the users who form the base of support for their suppliers, whose patronage accounts for the bulk of their earnings and profits, and whose needs define the nature of their businesses. As long as a business lives it must respond to its key accounts. If it stops, or if its key accounts find a greater responsiveness elsewhere, the business will die.

The art of staying in business as a viable supplier is the art of acquiring and holding key accounts. Because they are so special, a special strategy must be adopted to serve them. Such a strategy must go far beyond the provision of high-quality products which are delivered on time under fair, competitive terms. It must transcend the provision of gratuitous services, free goods, price offers, and other philanthropic tactics that can erode profit and professional sales management at one and the same time.

KEY-ACCOUNT PROBLEM AREAS

The requirements of a key-account strategy are far easier stated than met. This is because key accounts exist in a context which is chock full of tough, inflexible problems that began to take shape in the decade of the 1960s and that has become earmarked by the following major problem areas.

Increased product standardization. Most companies had discovered by the mid-1960s that innovation was a risky business. Research and development sometimes seemed to be a bottomless pit with huge sums of investment dollars going in and, for apparently endless periods of time, nothing coming out. Even when new product developments emerged from the R&D process, the odds were often estimated to be as high as eight or nine out of ten that they would fail commercially. As a result, companies turned to imitative marketing. It was easier, and certainly less costly or uncertain, to duplicate someone else's success. Making marginal renovations in an established product line was much more palatable than trying to take quantum jumps that would probably fail. Because competitors imitated each other's big winners, major product categories rapidly became standardized. Me-too products abounded. Salesmen, as a consequence, were progressively being deprived of product-superiority features to sell. With increasing frequency, there were few satisfactory product-oriented answers to the question, "Why should I buy from you?"

Accelerated competition from new materials and technologies. The electronics revolution has been a hallmark of the mid-twentieth century. As it has progressed, it has been steadily threatening older manufacturing and operating processes and inspiring new ones. Solid state overtook the transistor and the integrated circuit promised to overtake them both, even while some suppliers and their sales forces were still trying to convert their expertise from the electrical age. At the same time, plastics technology was maturing and becoming more versatile and more reliable. Industries from packaging to chemical processing felt its inroads as sales forces tried to learn either to sell plastics or to sell established materials defensively against them.

As jet power competed with piston power, hydraulic power with mechanical power, and electronic data processing power with manual power, customer options were multiplied hugely. In direct proportion, so were sales force problems. Old customer relationships, based on established materials and processes that both a salesman and his purchaser could easily understand, were being split asunder. Confusion was evident everywhere.

Protracted price erosion. Partly because of the new competition from recently developed materials and technologies, partly because of increasing product standardization caused by imitation, and partly because of both innovative and imitative competition from foreign suppliers in Europe and Asia, a protracted price erosion occurred over a broad spectrum of product lines. Profits were successively squeezed out of even successful sales transactions. In some cases, price lists changed with the calendar. In other cases, price lines were held, but hidden giveaways sweetened the deal. And in more cases than anyone cares to recall, price lists became jokes. In all these cases, price disintegration signaled the descent of once-premium brands into commodity status. Salesmen weaned on benefit-selling were frequently unable, or unwilling, to make the transition to price salesmanship. Those who were able to switch rather than fight made the recurring discovery that it would have cost their companies less to forsake many of their sales than to come away with them "successfully."

Insistent demands for customer service. When the prices of standardized products could not be further bargained down among alternate suppliers, increased free services were habitually demanded as a premium. Much of the time, too, enlarged technical and applications services have been truly necessary to help customers make the most economic or effective use of new materials and new processes. Salesmen found themselves becoming so deeply involved with their customers' operations that they were required to allocate greater amounts of time with each customer just to insure the successful use of the products or materials they had sold. A sale was no longer completed when the order was signed. Nor did a sale end when delivery took place or even when the invoice was paid. The sale ended only when the customer's customers expressed satisfaction with their own purchases, which, perhaps somewhere deep inside, contained the salesman's component or benefited from his applications skill. The concept of the *product and service system* was created as much in acknowledgment of this existing drain on selling time and talent as in recognition of a genuine market need. But for most salesmen and their managers, it still remained a system of selling as much product as possible and giving away as little service as required.

Stratified decision making. With purchase decisions becoming more complex and involving a variety of knowledge resources, purchasing teams and buying committees replaced the traditional one-to-one relationship of salesman and purchasing agent or salesman and design engineer. It was becoming all but impossible for a salesman to know the balance of decision-making power in the committee system. In many instances he could not even know who all the committee members were.

Salesmen came to realize that they now had many more influences to call on at each customer company. But they also quickly discovered that they had no natural interface with men who were marketing directors, new product developers, corporate planners, and the like. Access to these position holders was difficult, limited, and perilous. An unprepared salesman might gain entry to them once. But if he did not make a contribution, he might never be admitted again. And of course there was always the problem of finding time to penetrate a company in such depth and to prepare to deal persuasively with such a wide range of disciplines and personalities.

Much of the time it was easier to retreat to the purchasing department and, in an attempt to beat the system, try to get a friendly purchasing agent to play by the old rules. Even though this method rarely succeeded, it offered a nostalgic counterpoint to the new type of stratified decision making.

CONSULTATIVE SELLING AS A PROBLEM-SOLVING RESPONSE

Out of this background has come a sales strategy that promises to solve the problems that have been bedeviling product salesmanship, either by meeting the problems head-on or by outflanking them. Because the problems have created new customer needs that are bold departures from the past, the new strategy is bold too. It is the key-account strategy of *consultative selling,* an approach to creating long-term, mutually beneficial sales relationships with major customers by helping them improve their profit through the use of the salesman's products and services.

The normal problem-solving process that takes place in a key account is a four-step sequence. It originates with awareness of a specific problem in the customer's mind and ends with the delivery of a solution by a supplier. The sequence begins when the customer becomes aware that he has a problem. At this point he probably perceives the problem narrowly. He may think that he alone has the problem and that it has become his problem because his business is different. He does not see its generic nature. By reacting simplistically, he will probably not see the problem as having more than one cause. Nor does he usually foresee its potential ramifications. He only knows that he hurts. If one common attribute could be ascribed to him, it would be the cry, "Help!"

A customer's awareness that he has a problem can develop spontaneously. If it does, the consultative salesman's role is to give it a focus. If it does not, the salesman's role will be to stimulate it. The next stage in the customer's problem-solving sequence is the one that proves whether the consultative salesman has positioned himself properly. If he has, his customer will immediately become aware that the consultative salesman's company has the solution to his problem. Unless this awareness takes place, the consultative salesman will be unable to function as a problem solver. Under ideal conditions, a customer's awareness that the salesman's company has the solution will follow almost simultaneously upon awareness of the problem itself. When this occurs, it demonstrates that the consultative salesman has positioned himself in a professional manner. He has been able to rule out debate on the individual merits of his solution. He has also been able to isolate himself from competitive solutions.

In the third and fourth stages of the problem-solving process, the ball is in the supplier's court. The consultative salesman's roles are to lead the problem-solving actions inside his own company and then to apply the resulting solution to improve his customer's profit. These are the ways he adds value to his company's sales function and to his customer's earnings. As the International Business Machines Corporation says about its sales force, they "are not just out selling equipment. They are working with the top management of our customers, *helping them solve essentially management problems.*"

OPPORTUNITIES FOR CONSULTATIVE SELLING

The problem-solving approach of consultative selling has proved to be a highly cost-effective sales strategy for a broad and rather varied group of businesses. Most kinds of industrial, scientific, and technical products benefit from being sold consultatively. It is also becoming a virtual requirement of systems selling approaches where a product and its attendant services are bundled together or a number of compatible products are sold as a unit.

Data processing systems, fire protection and other safety and security systems, communications equipment and the heavy capital goods products sold for industrial construction, power generation and transmission, and environmental control are all best sold through consultative strategies. Packaging materials are being increasingly sold through consultative customer relationships. So are rather mundane products like refractory brick, whose salesmen now sell by consulting with furnace superintendents of steel and glass melters on the most cost-effective melting operations. Materials cleaning equipment salesmen operate in a similar manner. They consult with processors on improving the quality and profitability of their operations by utilizing the salesman's products, services, and personal expertise.

Since consultative selling is designed to convert a product-buying relationship into a customer-service business, it is natural that outright service suppliers in practically any field can improve their performance when they sell with a consultative method. Airlines are employing consultative selling strategies through their station agents. Bank loan officers and accountants are becoming consultative salesmen with key clients. So are dealers and distributors. In many industries, distributors are altering their sales mix to concentrate on educating and servicing their key accounts while the hardware sales they used to make are now being processed directly by their equipment suppliers.

Consultative selling fits these industries, along with a large number of others, because it helps solve one or more problems they all have in common. As a general rule, there are eight kinds of problems that, singly or in some combination, can make consultative selling a strategy of choice.

There are four major consultative selling opportunities resulting from problems within the salesmen's own business: (1) A supplier may require a means of creating a distinctive difference in his marketing strategies that will enable him to break away from competitive parity. (2) A supplier may require a means of restoring a commodity selling situation to a more preemptive branded sale. (3) A supplier may require a means of combating price erosion and regaining or justifying premium prices. (4) A supplier may require a means of introducing innovation into his business to relieve the burdens of products or services whose life cycles have become mature or moribund.

There are four major consultative selling opportunities resulting from problems within a key account's business: (1) A key account may require improved profitability by means of cost reduction in his current product lines or the growth of new earnings which must come from new product or new market development. (2) A key account may require expert applications knowledge or the infusion of new information into his processes, generally because of dynamic changes occurring in his technology or marketing base. (3) A key account may require the turnaround of a lagging aspect of his business or a revival of a dormant business. (4) A key account may require relief from inroads being made into his business by direct competitors or—even more serious—by indirect competitors from more aggressive industries.

CONSULTATIVE SELLING VERSUS PRODUCT SELLING

Consultative selling represents a day-and-night difference from product selling. It redefines the salesman and his job. It restructures his sales relationships. It repositions the sales function in the marketing mix to bring it more closely into line with the demands of the new selling environment of the 1970s in six principal ways.

1. The consultative salesman regards himself as the manager of his own personal service business. He treats his accounts not as customers but as *clients*. In this role, he has two objectives: to help them maximize the profitable operation of their business and thereby to maximize the profitable operation of his own.

2. As a business manager of a personal service business, the consultative salesman is concerned with the sum total of his clients' needs which his combined personal and corporate expertise can help make more efficient or more economical. As a result, he is prepared to offer broad *systems of product and service benefits*. He does not give away services or provide them reluctantly. Nor does he regard services as simply a throwaway value added to his product sales, the parsley that surrounds the steak. Instead, he promotes services vigorously and markets them at a profit that is often greater than his profit from product sales.

3. The consultative salesman is a *marketer*. This means that his primary concern is with the markets of his key accounts, since they are the base on which the account's business is built. For him to know a customer's business in terms of its processing and distribution systems is not enough. He must also know *the business of his customer's customers*. To be able to say about a consultative salesman that he "really knows the pulp and paper business" means that he knows the needs of its key customers, the problems that create their needs, and the solutions that key customers will most readily accept.

4. The consultative salesman concentrates on *profitable sales*. Unlike many product salesmen whose motto is always "sell more," the consultative salesman avoids the temptations of increased dollar sales, higher volume sales, or sales to expand a share of market except when these achievements can make a significant contribution to profit. His principal concern is with managing not the largest possible business but the most profitable business. For this reason the consultative salesman may not offer

service to, or may reject requests for service from, unprofitable or perhaps even marginally profitable customers. By the same token, he may defer trying to solve some customer problems merely because they are solvable. Instead, he will concentrate only on the problems that are most profitable for him to solve.

5. The consultative salesman is a *business planner.* He plans not just his major customer calls but his entire business relationship with his key customers. His business plans are mostly short range. As he strings them together in sausage-like links, he moves into the long range of each customer's business. It is

Figure 1.1   The consultative sales approach versus traditional product selling.

Performance Requirements of the Consultative Salesman	Performance Requirements of the Product Salesman
Performs a profit improvement planning function for his customer-clients and for their own key customers	Performs a product-supply planning function for his customers.
Helps customers define their businesses, their markets, and their product and service systems.	Helps customers acquire and apply his company's products.
Maintains wide, multifunction access inside his customer companies and their own key customers.	Maintains access principally with customer purchasing and engineering functions.
Sells systems of services and products, with primary emphasis on services.	Sells products and closely related product-application services, with primary emphasis on products.
Draws on a full complement of his company's functions and services for his support.	Draws principally on sales and technical services for his support.

through this planning partnership with his customers that he embeds himself, together with his product and service systems, in their businesses.

6. The consultative salesman is an *innovator*. He seeks out customer needs for new product and service systems and new markets. Then he actively presides over combined customer–supplier approaches to anticipating these needs and satisfying them.

Figure 1.1 summarizes the principal ways in which the consultative sales approach differs from traditional product selling.

MULTIFUNCTION CUSTOMER ACCESS AND MULTIRESOURCE SERVICE CAPABILITIES

The consultative salesman's wide-ranging access within his customer organizations is based on two unique assets: (1) his systems capability, and (2) his "branded" business management skills in putting his systems to work for each customer's profit improvement.

As Figure 1.2 shows, a consultative salesman may relate to as many as four major customer functions: marketing, sales, technology, and finance. Within these functional classifications, over a dozen individual position titles may be among his regular and occasional contacts. At each contact level the consultative salesman has two duties to perform. He must manage the application of his own personal expertise and his company's product and service systems to improve his customer's profit potential. And he must communicate his customer's major needs back to his company. In this way, his company will always have sufficient knowledge and lead time to develop preemptive systems for serving customer needs with the greatest economy and efficiency.

Every customer contact will demand a different set of primary capabilities from the consultative salesman. Many of these capabilities can be made available to his customer's key customers as well. To each contact, at least one capability will probably be universally offered: the information resource of the consultative salesman's company.

Without specific training for his new multifunctional tasks, no salesman can be expected to operate consultatively. He will not transform himself by simply calling himself a consultative salesman. Customers remain skeptical, and properly so, about the value of a surface transformation without much underlying substance. "The idea to serve us consultatively is a good one," they have often commented. "But we are not about to invite a salesman into our privy councils, make him a partner in our proprietary planning for the future, or even rely on his advice. How could we trust his wisdom? Or his confidence?"

Figure 1.2   The consultative salesman's range of potential customer relationships.

Customer Function	Customer Position Titles that May Be Related to by Consultative Salesman	Consultative Salesman's Capabilities that Form Basis of Relationship
Marketing	1. Chief Marketing Officer 2. Product or Brand Manager 3. Market Manager 4. Marketing Services Manager 5. Advertising Manager 6. Marketing Research Manager	Market development services to customers and jointly to customers' customers
Sales	1. General Sales Manager 2. Regional or District Sales Manager 3. Dealer or Distributor Sales Manager	Sales strategy development services and sales training services to customers and jointly to customers' customers
Technology	1. Research & Development Director 2. Product Development Managers and Development Engineers	Technological development services to customers and jointly to customers' customers
Finance	1. Controller 2. Corporate Planning Director	Profit-planning services to customers and jointly to customers' customers

POSITION DESCRIPTION OF THE CONSULTATIVE SALESMAN

The importance of the consultative salesman's involvement with his key accounts' planning processes, and thereby with their growth and development strategies, is paramount. For this reason, the responsibility for profit improvement planning has been given first place in the position description for the consultative salesman in the excerpt which appears as Figure 1.3. In second place are

Figure 1.3   Consultative salesman position description.

BASIC FUNCTION

The basic function of this position is to counsel within key customer organizations in improving the profit from their business planning in such a way that each account can be maintained and developed as a major contributor to company profit through the purchase and use of the most profitable mix of product and service systems marked by or through the company.

MAJOR RESPONSIBILITIES

The major responsibilities involved in fulfilling the basic function of this position are:

1. Profit Improvement Planning

The standard of performance for this responsibility is met when the consultative salesman is managing a joint company-account plan that coordinates the profit improvement needs of the account with the capabilities of the company, so that account needs can be anticipated and met at maximum profit to the company through marketing an optimal mix of products, services, and product-service systems.

To execute this responsibility, the consultative salesman will be required to define account business, markets, and product-service systems; forecast account needs and their schedules; improve the profitability of the account's business base through the application of company resources; and help insure the account's continuing improved profitability as a direct result of his counsel.

Figure 1.3   (continued)

---

2. Sales Contact and Communication

The standard of performance for this responsibility is met when the consultative salesman is creating the climate of confidence that enables him to maintain close and continuing contact and communication with key-account planning, developmental, marketing, technical, and purchasing decision makers—and their correlate functionaries within the account's key customer organizations—so that the planned mix of company products, services, and product-service systems is sold to and applied by the account in a manner and volume calculated to realize company short-term profit and long-term image objectives.

To execute this responsibility, the consultative salesman will be required to initiate and maintain professional consultative relations with account marketing, technical, and financial management, as well as the account's own key customer correlates, on the basis of shared information and expertise. This will enable the consultative salesman to negotiate profit improvement plans on behalf of the company as a true supplier–partner to the account.

PRIMARY ACCOUNTABILITY

As a member of the general sales management staff, the consultative salesman is primarily accountable to the general sales manager for the performance of his basic function and major responsibilities.

The general sales manager will measure the consultative salesman's accountability by:

1. The cost-efficiency of his operations, as measured by the manner in which he returns a maximum profit based on a minimal investment.

2. The quality of his account planning, as measured by the nature and degree of his close, continuing account involvement, the growth of his accounts' profit objectives, and the consistent achievement of these objectives.

3. The climate of confidence created in his account and company relationships, as measured by his personal acceptance and the preemptive importance he creates for his contribution in each of his principal interrelationships.

his direct sales contact and communication responsibilities. This order of responsibilities symbolizes one of the most significant differences between the consultative salesman and the product-line salesman.

A second significant difference lies in the consultative salesman's contact responsibilities. The product salesman principally confronts purchasing agents, buying committees, technical specifiers such as design engineers, and their influencers. The consultative salesman, in order to plan his own role and his company's role in his customers' business growth, must range widely and deeply within their organizations. This is because the consultative salesman sells broad yet closely related systems of services and products. His primary emphasis is on the service component of his systems approach. Because he can preempt a specialty capability for his services—that is, because he is able to brand them with his unique personal and corporate mix of capabilities—he is most likely to lead with his services and pull his products along as the hardware that naturally complements the service software.

THE DESIRED OUTCOMES

When a salesman is able to practice his art at a high enough level to negotiate a consultative selling situation with a key account, three interrelated outcomes generally identify the relationship. They affect the salesman's concept of his customers, the way he positions what he sells, and the master benefit he promotes.

Making customers into clients. One outcome of a consultative selling relationship is the transformation of the salesman's customers into clients. This is far more than just a semantic difference. A customer is someone to be sold; a client is someone to be served. In a consultative relationship the client wins all the time. He does not win *over* the salesman; he wins *with* him. He cannot lose because the salesman will not let him. What he wins is profit improvement. The salesman must win profit improvement too. His ultimate professional skill is to manage each consultative relationship so that both he and his client prosper. Because the co-prosperous nature of the consultative situation rewards the self-seeking needs of both members, it provides the best guarantee of its longevity.

The conversion process by which a customer becomes a client is a consultative salesman's most continuing and demanding task. It is his principal educational burden. Each of his customer relationships is a schoolroom in which his curriculum in elementary and advanced clienthood must be taught on a day-in and day-out basis. The salesman will be able to tell how well he is succeeding according to five major landmarks.

- A customer is a buyer of products. When he becomes a client, he will be a *consumer of services.*
- A customer is price sensitive. When he becomes a client, he will be *profit sensitive.*
- A customer is also competitor sensitive, with a keen awareness of the salesman's rivals. When he becomes a client, he will be *less sensitive to the salesman's competition.*
- A customer operates with the salesman within a relatively short time frame. When he becomes a client, he will operate within *a longer time frame.*
- A customer applies controls to the salesman's performance. When he becomes a client, he will *share the development of the relationship's controls* with the salesman.

Making product sales into service sales. A second outcome of a consultative selling relationship is that product sales are turned into the sale of what is essentially a problem-solving service to the client. The product does not need to be deemphasized in order to accomplish this objective. Instead, its hardware aspects must be translated into service benefits. In this sense, even a massive capital equipment sale can become an intangible transaction. To insure client satisfaction, a service system is usually constructed to surround each sale. Information is the principal service in each system. Then, complementing and supplementing it may be insurance services, leasing and financing services, and others. Marketing these beneficial services is a natural extension of regarding the customer as a client. If he remains positioned as a customer, the tendency to give these services away will probably be irresistible.

Making profit improvement the supreme service. In traditional selling situations the burden is generally on the salesman to justify purchase to his customers. In a consultative relationship this burden is multiplied many times over. There are two reasons why this is so. For one, a salesman who acts in the role of a consultant is constantly on trial. Since his promise is to solve customer problems by adding profit, it entails far more than the promise to supply a product. The magnified expectations and dependencies he generates must be fulfilled. There are few, if any, permissible excuses for failure. Second, the consultative salesman acts in a limited frame of reference. When all is said and done, there is usually only one justification for purchase which he can put forth. Either his proposed product and service system will work to improve a customer's profit or there is little reason for urging it upon him. His stringent profit orientation denies the salesman recourse to unquantifiable justifications and channels him into a true fiduciary relationship. This is the supreme manifestation of his service. It illuminates the interesting paradox that while the consultative salesman's sell is intangible, the measurable, countable profit which he must deliver is the most tangible outcome of all.

ANSWERS TO QUESTIONS SALESMEN ASK

Salesmen who read the consultative salesman's position description and study the desired outcomes from his performance frequently express one or more of four doubts. One is about their own capability to learn and employ consultative strategies. A second is about the degree of acceptance they can expect from their key accounts. A third is how consultative selling can be justified in terms of the major time investment it requires in an ever uncertain account relationship. The fourth is about what happens if everybody in an industry begins selling consultatively.

"How do we know we can become consultative salesmen?" is what salesmen often ask as they try to match their own perceived abilities with the strategies of the consultative approach. "How can we tell that we have what it takes?" The only way to know for certain, of course, is to apply consultative strategies to a key account. But even beforehand, a salesman can preview himself in a relatively straightforward manner by evaluating three aspects of his talent mix. His *motivation* comes first. Does he have the desire to develop professional knowledge about a customer's business, especially its manufacturing and marketing processes? *Dedication* is a second consideration. Does he have the concentration necessary to explore a wide range of optional ways to improve his customer's profit, knowing in advance that he will have to reject or rework most of them before he can hope to install them— and that, even then, he will have to monitor and measure their progress long after the excitement of their novelty has worn off? The third talent a salesman requires is the ability to achieve his own *self-actualization* largely through contributing to the enrichment of his customers.

Salesmen also want to know how their key accounts are likely to react to them when they make their opening consultative approach. "Will we have to motivate a customer to accept our new role?" "How do we get started: do we suddenly announce that from now on we are going to be consultative salesmen?" When the salesman tries for the first time to position himself consultatively with a key account, he may encounter reactions ranging from polite curiosity to skepticism. He will have to change his image with care and credibility. A good way to face the problem is to introduce the change something like this:

"Up to this point, my contribution to our relationship has been based on assuring you of a supply of quality products and product-related services which have been helpful to you in earning a profit on the sales you make to your customers. Now, I want to begin to emphasize my ability to improve your profit in a more systematic manner."

The response the salesman seeks is the question, "What is your plan?" "My plan," the salesman can then respond, "is to help you improve the profit on your sales of product X by 5%." When the customer asks the magic question, "How?," the salesman can begin to sell.

Because a consultative approach obviously requires a salesman to make a serious time commitment in his customer's business, salesmen want to know how to reconcile it with results. "Suppose we get ourselves deeply involved? What happens if we lose the account—how do we justify our investment?" By getting involved in his customer's plans through the promise of adding profit to them, a salesman is taking the single most effective step open to him to consolidate a long-term lasting relationship. Profit improvement is his best insurance policy against all but capricious account losses or those that occur for reasons removed from the salesman's interaction with his customer. By definition, key accounts are too valuable to lose. For this reason they are worth serving with the strategy that can help them the most and bind them the closest to their most helpful source of supply.

In selling, sauce for the goose soon becomes sauce for the gander. However unique it may be, no product and no sales strategy remains exempt from competitive imitation for very long. "Is this not also true of consultative selling?" salesmen often ask. "What happens when everybody is selling consultatively? Haven't we just escalated knock-off competition to a higher level of cost and complexity?" If consultative selling is going to become the standard key-account relationship in an industry, there is no doubt that each supplier will have to match his competitors by adopting it. The greatest rewards may go to the company that adopts it first.

But even if all suppliers copy each other's consultative systems approach identically, and even if each of them offers to plan profit improvement for his customers, consultative selling does not permit exact replication. This is because *it is a service and not a product.* Only products can be standardized. Services can always remain branded, and therefore unique, because of the personal nature of their application. All suppliers may offer consultative selling. But each customer account will prefer to deal with only one of them because of the particular human and operating values created by an individual salesman and his skill in applying his disciplines. It is the salesman's uniqueness which makes consultative selling operative and which insulates it from ever being neutralized by rival suppliers. In the final analysis, the supreme added value offered by selling consultatively is the personal service of the salesman himself.

2/Customer Relations Strategies

A PRODUCT SALESMAN can sell as long as his customer has a minimal level of confidence in the product. A consultative salesman can sell his product and service systems only if a customer has a high level of confidence in the salesman. Creating a climate of confidence in which he can function consultatively is the key to building a profitable customer relationship. It is also the most important and the most difficult of the three disciplines of consultative selling.

Confidence-building is the most important discipline because a salesman cannot consult without his customer's permission. Confidence is the source of this permission. Confidence-building is the most difficult discipline because it makes four tough demands on the salesman: he must perceive himself accurately; he must perceive his customers correctly in the key accounts where he will be selling; he must make accurate perceptions about the value system, the communication and decision-making system, and the power structure of his customers' organizations; and he must learn how to deal with his customers and their systems by means of a give-and-take, no-win and no-lose process of negotiation. These areas of perception and learning are the salesman's building blocks for the climate of confidence he must create.

Most salesmen probably have had the pyramid shown in

Figure 2.1 permanently engraved on their consciousness. Because, on the surface, personal objectives can appear similar among many customers and, after a while, even their buying behavior may seem predictable, salesmen may be inclined to deal with the samenesses among customers rather than their differences. Yet the individual traits which make every man like no other man are the real determinants of success for the salesman who wants to sell consultatively.

Ritualistic sales techniques that concentrate on common human traits or even group traits, and that work well enough in product selling situations, are of little use to a consultative sales-

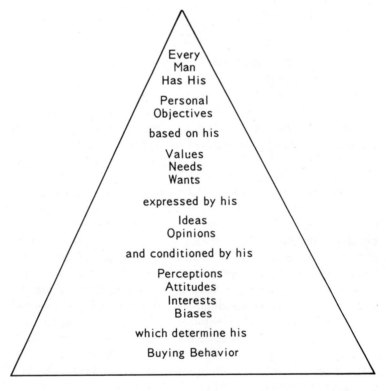

Figure 2.1 The personal objectives/buying behavior pyramid.

man. His is an intensely personal relationship. To make it even more complicated, it is also extremely diverse. The consultative salesman regularly must go one-on-one with many different decision makers and influencers in his key accounts. Not only are their job titles different. So are their backgrounds, their experience, and their expectations about a salesman and his role. A sizable number of them have no history of ever dealing with a salesman. They have no more idea of how to interact with him than he may have of them. Automatic behavior on his part is quickly self-defeating. Without the ability to know each other, each must rely on his perceptions.

Superficially, perception is simple. It is the process of getting to know what is "out there." We gather what we sense is the reality of a situation, organize it, and use it as the basis of our interactions with others who share the situation with us. Because the easiest bits of information for us to pick up about each other are the behavioral cues which our senses relay to us, our perceptions are far more likely to be subjective than objective. They are also more emotional than rational, somewhat incomplete, and more or less inaccurate. On the basis of our perceptions we form our impressions of reality. In our unreal "real world," what we believe to be facts may be fiction; what we believe to be fiction may be facts. Nonetheless, *what we perceive is what is real for us.*

To sell consultatively therefore requires the salesman to be an accurate perceiver. The real world he senses in his customer relationships must be more fact than fiction. Otherwise his relationship will be profitless. To equip himself to perceive accurately and realistically, a consultative salesman requires the ability to practice five skills: (1) sensitivity to cues sent forth by his customers; (2) interpreting them correctly; (3) integrating them into a meaningful picture of each customer; (4) responding appropriately to customer stimuli; and (5) having available an armory of flexible strategies for relating to each customer's individual differences.

The initial task of each consultative salesman is to use his skills for one objective: to understand each of his key-account correlates who influence the confidence level of his selling climate. Therefore, the salesman must try to

> *Think with* his customer . . . not for or about him
> *Feel with* his customer . . . not become emotionally involved
> *Move with* his customer . . . not rush ahead or lag behind
> *Relate to* his customer . . . not be either friend or foe
> *Work with* his customer . . . not work for or against him
> *Accept* his customer . . . not judge or criticize him
> Help his customer *satisfy his needs* . . . not just the needs of the salesman

These are abilities and attitudes which a consultative salesman must learn, for in most cases they do not come naturally. Quite often, they go against the grain of the salesman's accustomed way of doing things. There may even be times when they violate thoughts, feelings, and satisfactions that are paramount in his mind. By understanding how personalities function in a consultative situation and how to perceive opportunities to deal successfully with the needs they generate, the salesman can get off on the right foot in his key customer relations.

BUILDING A CLIMATE OF CONFIDENCE

When a consultative salesman and his customer consult together, their interactions will be influenced by ten principles that govern how they perceive each other.

PRINCIPLES OF SALESMAN–CUSTOMER PERCEPTION

The principles of perception which have direct application to the consultative selling relationship affect the degree and type of confidence that earmarks it. These principles concern the perceptions that do business with each other, the personalized nature of perception, the importance of initial impact, the chain reaction effect of trait linkage, perceptual unity, the importance of cognitive structure, and the overriding value of self-understanding as the basis for perception.

Perceptions, not people, do business. Salesmen and their customers normally adopt a first-person viewpoint with each other. Each reacts not to the reality of a situation but to the manner in which he sees it. He will twist, distort, and modify the reality to make it understandable to himself. What is more, he will probably do so unintentionally and unconsciously. These unconsciously modified perceptions are the ones that do business with each other.

Perception is a personalized process. A salesman perceives what is significant to him. To do so he scans, searches, sorts, filters, blocks, and selects from among the fast-flowing stimuli in a sales situation only those that make sense to him and that fit in with his often preconceived notions. In this way, perception becomes his process of satisfying needs. When his needs are great, what the salesman "sees" will be greatly influenced by them. In the same way, the customer will also be influenced by his own needs. Canned presentations ignore customer needs. So does a salesman who relies too much on past dealings which appear on their surface to be identical with his present situation.

Initial impact is important. Every salesman knows that he must make a positive first impression. Not all salesmen know why. According to the rule of primacy, the characteristics which a customer first perceives in a salesman tend to be lasting. These first impressions serve a steering and gate-ing function, acting as a sieve which allows later impressions to get through while screening out most others. In this way, first impressions become lasting. They also grow on themselves. All of us search for additional evidence that substantiates our first impressions. It is always available. When we find it, we experience a self-fulfilling prophecy.

Once a customer sees a salesman as incompetent, it will be very difficult for him to alter his initial reading. At every hint of personal or professional incompetence which the salesman gives, the customer's first impression will be reinforced. Even if the salesman displays competence, the customer will tend to discount it and will return to collecting cues that enable him to go on regarding the salesman as incompetent. Competence is therefore as much in the eye of his beholders as it is in the salesman's own performance.

A way of perceiving is also a way of not perceiving. Every salesman has his own implicit theory of personality based on his own ideas, however inaccurate they may be, of the way people should and should not act. Once he perceives certain traits in a customer, his implicit personality theory takes over. This is the same mind-setting process that goes on in his customer. The salesman must therefore be on guard against allowing his own first impressions and personality theory to prevent him from seeing his customer as an individual human being.

One good trait deserves another. Through a mental structuring process known as trait linkage, a customer who attributes one good trait to a salesman will also tend to attribute other good traits. A salesman who is regarded as being helpful is also likely to be thought of as smart and interested in the customer's business. The opposite kind of linkage also occurs. A salesman who is slow is easy to classify as unsure of himself, inexperienced, or a crafty man who looks both ways before he sticks his neck out because he doesn't like to commit himself.

Perceptions are unified and not modular. The perception that one man has of another is usually a single, overall generalization. It is selectively organized as a unit and is thought of in this way, rather than in terms of the modules which compose it. This habit tends to make perceptions black or white, not gray. We rarely see both sides of a story. We configure it in one way or another despite internal inconsistencies which we may nevertheless readily admit to.

Attraction begets attraction. In consultative selling, familiarity cannot be allowed to breed contempt. It must lead to an ever improving relationship. The easiest relationships to initiate and nurture are those in which a salesman and his customer share characteristics that each accepts in himself. In such a relationship the salesman and his customer will readily be able to like each other. When this occurs, each will be inclined to perceive the other as being more like him than he really is. This is based on the human trait that makes us perceive more accurately the ways in which someone is similar to us and to overemphasize their importance. In consultative selling, opposites do not attract. As soon as a customer dislikes a salesman, he will tend to perceive all the ways in which he is different and to exaggerate their importance. At the same time, he will perceive far less accurately any ways in which they may be similar.

Everyone perceives according to his cognitive structure. Neither the consultative salesman nor his customers are blank pages on which each can write as he chooses. Both are already written on. The pages contain each man's cognitive structure, which operates in a highly predictable manner. The characteristics that each man considers to be the most important aspects of himself will predominate in forming his initial impressions of the other man. The categories that each man uses in describing his favorite qualities serve as the chief bench marks which regulate his descriptions of the other man. If a salesman unwittingly imposes his personal frame of reference on his customers, as he perceives them, he will have only himself to blame if his customers react in a less than enthusiastic manner. Each customer has his own rules for perceiving that govern what he sees. By understanding them, the salesman will be able to restrain intrusions by his own ego onto what his customers should do and thereby improve his patience in dealing with them.

Figures 2.2 and 2.3 illustrate the difficulty we encounter when we are challenged to restructure the silent organization of our frames of reference in order to solve a problem. Figure 2.2

Figure 2.2   Perceptual challenge.

shows nine dots arranged in a rectangle. They must all be connected with no more than four interconnected straight lines drawn in one continuous stroke. The pen cannot be raised from the paper. As Figure 2.3 shows, the problem cannot be solved by staying within the rectangular structure that the original perception of the nine dots has imposed. Unless this silent constraint can be broken, what is known as the coerciveness of configuration will win over creative problem solving. This is the peril of a rigid frame of reference. Once a frame of reference can be broken enough to allow the rectangle's boundaries to be demolished so it can be restructured into an arrow head, solution is simple.

The ability to judge others is a complex skill. No one is a universal good judge of people. The process of estimating others is extremely complicated. The salesman's ability to judge is largely a function of his own willingness to be open and candid. If he can create an easy and natural style, devoid of tricks and gimmicks, he will find it easier to "read" his customers since they will be inclined to match his openness.

Self-understanding makes it easier to perceive others. A salesman who is aware of his own personality characteristics will make fewer errors in perceiving his customers accurately. He will

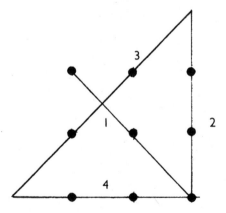

Figure 2.3 Perceptual creativity.

also be less inclined to judge his customers in extreme terms. The more aware he is about himself, the more secure he can be. This allows him to perceive others as being warm and accessible rather than cold and threatening. By regarding his customers more positively than negatively, the salesman who knows himself can quickly engender the kind of responsive behavior in his customer relations that can result in a fertile climate for sales.

OPENING THE PERCEPTIVE GATES

Perception is a process of *gate-ing*. As soon as the salesman perceives certain characteristics in his customer, gates automatically open in his mind which enable him to perceive similar characteristics. On the other hand, some gates automatically close. Unless he deliberately strives to open these gates, he will be unable to perceive the customer as a unique individual. The customer, in turn, is obviously working under a similar set of gate-ing limitations. What A sees in B is largely a function of what B sees in A. This perceptual reciprocity builds up as a cycle of understanding or misunderstanding.

Salesman Smith gets a picture of Customer Jones. Smith behaves toward Jones on the basis of this perception. Jones also has a picture of Smith and behaves toward him on this basis.

But neither Smith nor Jones is aware of the manner in which the other perceives him, much less the implicit personality theory on which each is operating. Each acts largely on the basis of his perception. Ironically, neither can know directly how the other perceives him. All that Smith and Jones observe is their interactive behavior.

Under these conditions, it is quite easy for Jones to direct his behavior toward a Smith which Smith does not acknowledge himself to be. The same thing, of course, applies to Smith in his dealings with Jones.

Once evolved, a cycle of misunderstanding can easily become intensified. Unless the salesman realizes that his customer is responding not to him as an individual but rather to his own perceptions of the salesman, their relationship can lead to a *reign of error*. It is not that their perceptions will pass each other like ships in the night. It is more likely that they will be on a collision course. Yet both parties will remain unaware of this fact until they experience the crunch of conflict.

PERCEPTUAL PITFALLS

Although the entire process of perception is loaded with traps, the consultative salesman must be especially wary of four pitfalls: stereotyping his customers, projecting his own failings onto customers, perceptual defense, and halo.

Stereotyping. Stereotyping attributes a group's general characteristics to an individual. Stereotypes may be negative or positive. Either way, they encourage the salesman to prejudge a customer by shortcutting the perceptual process of getting to know him. Stereotyping allows the salesman to profess advance knowledge. It may actually prevent perceptual understanding from occurring since the salesman will tend to screen his cues through the preselecting mechanism of his stereotypes. Only cues that agree will slip through.

Projection. Projection takes one of two forms. It can refer to the act of making others appear responsible for our mistakes. We all know how the poor workman blames his tools. The salesman who fails to make a sale may blame his company, his product, his competitors, or the customers he has to call on. A second form of projection is the habit of attributing our own faults to others.

Perceptual defense. When we are confronted with an experience that seems inconsistent with our cognitive structure, our first impulse is to maintain the cognitive structure. We accomplish this by ignoring, denying, or distorting the threatening experience. Ignoring a threat to our frame of reference is the easiest defense. If we ignore it, maybe it will go away. If it doesn't go away, we may have to explain it away with a rationale that is compatible with our reference framework. If we cannot rationalize it, we may be tempted to deny it or distort it. "That can't be the case," we say. "It just doesn't make sense." When these three defenses fail, we have to admit the incongruity of the situation. Only then can we integrate the new experience into our frame of reference. In this way, our stereotypes undergo slow and reluctant change as our perceptual growth occurs.

Halo. When we allow a general impression of a man to influence our judgment of his specific qualities, we are coloring our judgments with a halo effect. If our general impression is favorable, then the halo of specific characteristics we endorse him with will be mistakenly high. The reverse happens when our general impression is unfavorable. By advising a salesman to make a positive first impression on a customer, the objective is to create a positive halo.

To prepare for a first-impression meeting, it will be important for the salesman to know enough about his customer to perceive what his predispositions are. If the customer is predisposed to be introverted in his reactions to others, the salesman will have to be cautious not to act in an extremely extroverted manner unless he wants to be fitted for a negative halo. He will have to mute his assertiveness, relax his handshake, soften his voice and avoid fast talking, and in general restrain his impulsiveness in thought and action.

PERCEPTUAL ROLE ALTERATION

Each of us engages in two kinds of behavior. The first is our out-of-role behavior. We exhibit this behavior when we are not living up to the requirements of our job. The other is our in-role behavior. The professional roles we play are a reflection of how we expect others will expect a man in our role to behave. First we perceive the image of the role, then we tailor our behavior to fit the image. Eventually, the professional image becomes the professional man.

Most of our time and effort is invested in maintaining our behavior in keeping with our image of what it ought to be. A salesman is a man who does things like this or who looks like this, we say, and then we act accordingly. In a consultative relationship, a salesman cannot continue to act like a traditional salesman. Nor can he allow his customer to continue to play the traditional role that he perceives a customer should play. To bring about the transformation of roles that a consultative relationship requires, the salesman will have to educate himself and his customer in perceptual role alteration.

To operate as a successful consultant, the salesman-as-consultant must relate to the customer-as-client. As the salesman grows more accomplished in his role, the customer will come to perceive him more as a consultant than as a salesman. This transformation is a major index of the salesman's accomplishment. He must succeed in a second perceptual alteration as well. The customer must come to regard himself more as a client than as a customer.

The consultative salesman must become the agent for this role change. It will involve a learning experience in which the consultant must take a leadership position as a teacher. But he cannot teach down to his customer. He will have to teach across so that the learning experience can be shared rather than imposed. To say the same thing in another way, the salesman must lead the customer to new knowledge but must encourage him to digest it and apply it for himself. Only in this way can the customer incorporate what he learns into his behavior as a partner in joint achievement.

The central expectation that governs all consultative relationships is that they will be partnerships in growth. The customer must therefore be able to see the consulting salesman as someone who can add a sufficient value of new growth to exceed his cost. Perceiving added value generates the customer's motivation to enter the relationship and give the salesman access to him. Perceiving that the value exceeds its cost provides the customer's justification to allow the relationship to continue.

To play the role as a value adder, the consultative salesman must change his customer's perception of him from product supplier to problem solver and profit improver. These are consultant roles. He must then set about to change his customer's self-perception of his own role from objection raiser and price reducer to fellow problem solver and profit improver. These are client roles. Because they are common to consultant roles, a true partnership is possible for the consultative salesman and his customer which is hardly ever available to the product salesman.

PERCEPTIVE PERSONALITY PROFILING

Understanding ourselves is a difficult skill. Understanding others is no less difficult. Not only does the consultative salesman have to defend against his own stereotypes, frames of reference, projections, and halo effects, he must also penetrate the role-playing defenses of his customers.

In order to learn how to "read" his key-account correlates, the salesman must act as a combined participant-observer in his consultative relationships. As a participant, the salesman will be involved with his customer in a close, shared experience. Neither he nor the customer will be able to think or act independently of the other. That is why, in his role as observer, the salesman must disengage himself as much as possible from involvement with his customer so that he can note the full range of cues which enable him to carry on his work effectively.

For this reason, the salesman in a consultative relationship will find himself moving back and forth between a subjective participation in the relationship and an objective observation of its operations. He will have to rely on decentered rather than centered thinking so that he can take the customer's cues into account, screen out the trivial many, and focus on the vital few that enable him to profile perceptively the customer's personality. Personality profiling can give the salesman a major working tool: It will help him predict the actions his customers are most likely to take in given situations. To achieve this degree of advance understanding of his customers, the salesman will have to learn the principles of perceptive profiling and then how to apply them to his customers' cognitive style, conative structure, socioemotional traits, and their systems of values, interests, and attitudes.

PRINCIPLES OF PERCEPTIVE PROFILING

In his day-to-day operations with a key account, the consultative salesman requires only the use of his eyes and ears to perceive the critical aspects of each customer's personality and organization style that he should profile. He requires no unusual psychological expertise. What he must do is follow the fundamental principles of perception that will help him make his observations, move about inside his customer organizations, cultivate allies, apply understanding to his observations rather than judgment, maintain an intelligence file, formulate and test useful hypotheses, and create appropriate strategies from them.

Observe. Observation is the simplest principle of perception to put into practice. All the salesman has to do is watch and listen. Yet observation can also be difficult. This is because the salesman must carry on his watching and listening with empathy. Observation requires concentrated, disciplined attention to the cues and signals sent out by the customer. It also requires the salesman to have great patience for attending to detail. The major problem that the salesman must overcome is failing to see clearly what is really out there and, instead, perceiving only what he needs or wants to see. The salesman's own *selective inattention* is his worst potential enemy. It can lead him to make self-fulfilling prophecies by allowing him to see only what he looks for and then encouraging him to use it to substantiate his original expectation.

Get around. A consultative salesman must penetrate deeply and widely throughout his customer organization. He must become a master of the art of crossing organizational lines without making the organization's leaders cross. Only by getting around can the salesman hope to identify the key power figures who influence or determine the decision-making process. Beyond knowing who they are, he must make himself known to them as a problem solver who can help improve organizational profit. It is not enough that the salesman be known or even well known. He must become known *for* something. The best "something" to be known for is the benefit of profit improvement that he can offer.

Make alliances. As he broadcasts his benefit offering of improved profit throughout the influential areas of his customer's organization, the consultative salesman acts as an advertiser for himself. The customer organization is his medium. Like all advertisers, he must acquire testimonials in his favor from within the

organization. These testifiers can then become his internal sponsors. The salesman must therefore make alliances with key influencers in his key accounts. He must be careful to choose them
not just by title or function but by their ability to exert favorable
influence on his behalf and translate back to him their own perceptions of the assets and liabilities of his selling situation. If he selects them well and learns their own frames of reference, his allies
can act as extra pairs of eyes and ears for him which will multiply
his access throughout their organization.

Understand, don't judge. A salesman who allows himself
to become emotionally involved with his customers so that he begins to feel sympathetically in favor of or against them, instead
of empathetically with them, will find himself playing judge. He
will choose sides, moralize, be opinionated. As soon as this happens his objectivity is gone, and with it goes his chance to make
accurate perceptions. The consultative salesman must try to re-
strict his involvement to the level at which understanding takes
place, not judgment. He will always have his own preferences and
prejudices about customers. But the extent to which he can subordinate them in order to experience his customers without evaluating them will play a large part in determining his success.

Analyze. It is a good idea for a consultative salesman to
record his customer and organizational observations in a diary.
This can serve as his intelligence file. In it he can record current
perceptions of the individual strengths and weaknesses of key decision makers and influencers along with their blind spots, hypersen-
sitive areas, personality traits, preferences and aversions, overt and
hidden power lines, and other important data. For each customer
department the salesman can make a simple sociogram which con-
nects each key customer to his organizational supporters, antago-
nists, and neutrals. The salesman can also chart the interactions
between customer departments as well as who relates to whom
and how. Fortified with such analytical intelligence information,
the salesman will have a stronger base from which to create useful
hypotheses and to test them.

Create and test hypotheses. The salesman will have to tie
together the wide range of perceptions he picks up in order to

give them unity and coherence. A unified statement of this kind gives order to what he otherwise might pass off as unrelated perceptions. By combining them into a hypothetical explanation of a customer's personality or the organizational style of a key account, the salesman has an opportunity to inspect what his perceptions seem to be adding up to, confirm it by putting it to a test, or modify it by gathering additional evidence that will revise or refine it. Testing each hypothesis by putting it into limited action on a trial basis will help the salesman be certain that he is making it fit the facts rather than allowing himself to perceive only those facts that fit his hypothesis.

Evaluate hypotheses. The salesman must act as a manager of his perceptions. This means he must set up a businesslike set of controls to help him monitor his hypotheses and calculate their effect when he applies them to a customer. If an initial hypothesis proves unsuccessful, the salesman will have to go back to the drawing board and restructure it until it works. The criterion for a successful hypothesis is that it enables the salesman to deal with a customer's personality or organization in a climate of confidence.

PROFILING A CUSTOMER'S COGNITIVE STYLE

To "read" a customer, the first step a consultative salesman must take is to diagnose his cognitive style. This will enable him to learn how the customer receives, processes, stores, and utilizes the information that composes his frame of reference. Four aspects of cognitive style are important to analyze. Two of them are relatively simple to understand: the customer's speed of comprehension and his intellectual focus on abstract ideas, on more practical problems, or away from ideas and problems and onto people. Two other aspects of cognitive style are more complicated. They are the customer's cognitive complexity and his cognitive structure.

Cognitive complexity. Some customers have simple thought processes. Others are more complex. Three types of cognitive structure are useful for the consultative salesman to distinguish:

- Simplistic. Prefers either-or thought patterns, with information processed in polar opposite terms such as "good" or "bad."

- Orderly. Prefers disciplined, orderly thought patterns, with data sorted according to well-known and traditional categories.
- Complex. Prefers to analyze data along many dimensions accommodating a wide range of subtleties and nuances.

Cognitive structure. Customers differ in their cast of mind. Some are verbally oriented while others are primarily figure-oriented. One may be thoughtful and reflective while another will be unconventional and action-oriented. A simple way for the consultative salesman to profile two of his customers is illustrated in Figure 2.4. According to the figure, the salesman's approach to each of these customers must be markedly different. Customer B is mentally quick, comfortable with abstract ideas, but not unusually fast to act. His human relations perceptions are not outstand-

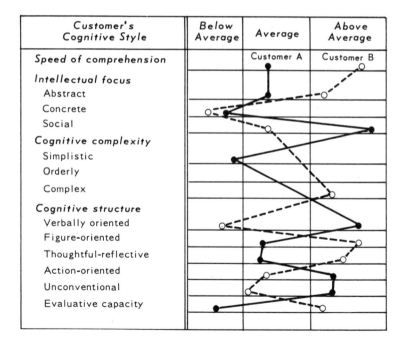

Figure 2.4 Cognitive structure profile.

ing. In addition, he is sharp and complex in his thinking and possesses acute evaluative abilities. He will give a poorly prepared salesman a hard time. On the other hand, customer A relates well but has no great preference for abstractions. He catches on slowly and tends to process information in polar terms. Verbally strong, he finds figures a bother and his evaluative capacity leaves something to be desired. In contrast to customer B, however, A is action-oriented and somewhat unconventional in his thinking. Simple, direct, forceful presentations meet his needs. What B might find boring, A may well find interesting. Yet the salesman may have to prod B to act, a possibility that is remote in dealing with A, who may have to be held back or redirected to on-target behavior.

PROFILING A CUSTOMER'S CONATIVE TENDENCIES

Customers are striving, seeking, acquisitive individuals. They are always doing something to satisfy their needs. There are six aspects about customer behavior that the consultative salesman should therefore bear in mind: (1) It is always caused and never random. (2) It is always goal-directed, even when its objective seems obscure. (3) It is always tension-reducing in the short run, even when it may create greater difficulty over the long term. (4) It always seeks either to increase need satisfaction or to avoid decreasing it. (5) It is never the result of only one drive or need. (6) It always appears perfectly reasonable to the customer at the time.

Since all customer behavior is need-satisfying in purpose, the consultative salesman should familiarize himself with a working knowledge of two major need theories: Maslow's theory and the approach of McClelland and White.

Maslow's theory.[1] Maslow has organized five human needs as a hierarchy, ranging from physiological needs such as food and clothing at the bottom through security needs, social needs, ego needs for achievement and respect, and self-actualization needs.

---

[1] A. H. Maslow, *Motivation and Personality* (New York: Harper & Brothers, 1954).

Maslow's hierarchy of needs suggests seven applications by a consultative salesman with a customer:

1. A salesman can motivate a customer only by appealing to the pattern of his needs that is currently dominant.
2. A customer will usually want a balanced satisfaction of all his needs rather than the maximum satisfaction of any single need.
3. Once a customer's need is satisfied, it will no longer motivate him.
4. Customer behavior is generally multimotivated.
5. The lower the level of a customer need, the easier it is to meet.
6. Most customers tend to emphasize the satisfaction of their higher-level needs.
7. Customers are insatiable so far as their need satisfaction is concerned. This is why customers ask, "What have you done for me lately?"

McClelland's and White's approaches. McClelland[2] and White[3] approach customers as achievers, men who are striving for accomplishment. They divide them into success seekers and failure avoiders. Success seekers prefer situations where the risk of failure is neither too great nor too small. They are motivated more by the prospect of achievement than by fear of failing. Failure avoiders prefer sure things, at one extreme or perhaps "chancey" things, at the other. They prefer situations that are predictable or those where luck, chance, or external variables can determine the outcome.

Since a success seeker and a failure avoider have different attitudes toward mastering situations, overcoming difficulties, and manipulating ideas, the consultative salesman will have to take a different tack with each of them. In Figure 2.5 the conative tendencies of two customers are profiled. Customers A and B are both success seekers. Yet in many other tendencies they are quite different. For example, customer B is likely to be the harder man

---

[2] D. C. McClelland, *The Achieving Society* (Princeton, N.J.: D. Van Nostrand Company, 1961).
[3] R. W. White, "Motivation Reconsidered: The Concept of Competence," *Psychological Review,* Vol. 66, No. 5, 1959.

to work with. His demands are probably rigorous since his concern for self-esteem, adequacy, status, and prestige are so high. Customer A has fewer extreme characteristics. He likes to take risks but his need for ego-building indicates that he will look for the salesman's aid and advice as support.

PROFILING A CUSTOMER'S SOCIOEMOTIONAL TRAITS

Because all human beings are social beings, a customer's socioemotional characteristics can be profiled across a wide range

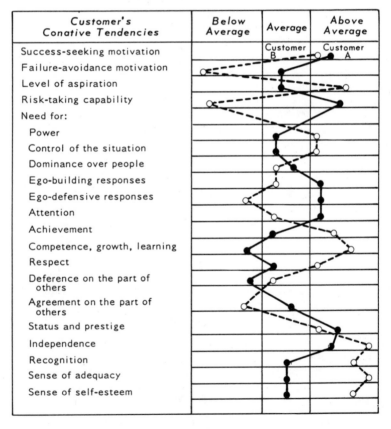

Figure 2.5   Conative tendency profile.

of attributes. As Figure 2.6 shows, they can be mapped in a way that reveals them clearly and in a simple summary form. The figure shows a comparison between customers A and B in six key attributes. Of the two men, A is likely to be more compatible with the salesman's attempts to involve him. He is also less self-assured and emotionally less mature. These traits may make him more changeable and flexible, although less dependable. Customer B,

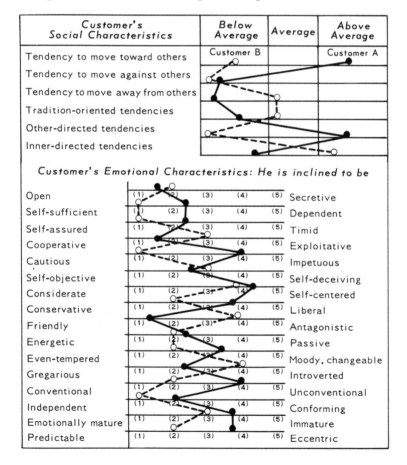

Figure 2.6 Social and emotional characteristics profile.

on the other hand, is harder to get to or involve but more dependable to work with.

PROFILING A CUSTOMER'S VALUES, INTERESTS, AND ATTITUDES

All customers have sets of values which condition their acceptance of the salesman and his relationship with them. A *value* is simply an ideal. An *interest* is a preference. An *attitude* is a predisposition to feel or act; sometimes it is called a mental set, indicating that the mind is set to go off in a certain direction that will determine action. The salesman should keep in mind the following six characteristics of the attitudes his customer can bring to a consultative relationship or may derive from it:

1. Attitudes are remarkably stable. Once formed, they are very difficult to change.
2. Attitudes defy logic. They often exist simply because they exist.
3. A customer may have contradictory attitudes.
4. Attitudes underlie a customer's motivation.
5. Attitudes determine a customer's perception of the salesman and his relationship with him.
6. Attitudes cannot be reasoned with. An appeal to "be reasonable" gains little or nothing in altering an attitude.

The consultative salesman has two simultaneous tasks when it comes to perceiving a customer's values, interests, and attitudes. First, he must profile his own. This will help him perceive himself more clearly. Second, he must learn how to detect his customer's values and attitudes even though a customer will rarely proclaim them. The customer's *behavior* will offer major clues. The customer's *communication,* especially what he connotes by leaving unsaid, will provide the salesman with his second set of clues. Chance comments, so-called offhand remarks which are really on-hand, silent comments, jokes, and opinions or evaluations which seemingly refer to others all reveal a customer's likes, dislikes, preferences, and aversions. A third set of clues can come from his customer's *expressed ideas* about issues, groups, and individuals. The salesman can use a simple checklist to profile the values, interests, and positive and negative attitudes which he perceives through observing and working with his customers.

PERCEPTIVE ORGANIZATION PROFILING

The customer is a part of the culture medium of his organization. The organization is also a part of the customer. A purchasing agent, design engineer, or product manager is a spokesman for a complex group of organizational pushes and pulls. As buying committees and steering committees grow in popularity among companies, the independence of each individual member diminishes because his own traits, values, and attitudes become colored by others. Knowing who these other influencers and decision makers are, as well as what personal and organizational points of view they represent, is essential for a salesman who wants to sell consultatively.

Unless he penetrates widely and deeply throughout his customer's organization, the salesman will find that he may encounter other problems as well. Because organizational changes are occurring more rapidly than ever before, events may make the salesman's original concept of a customer organization obsolete unless he keeps on top of them. As a result, he may encounter the "phantom organization" phenomenon of trying to deal with an organizational structure and a social system that no longer exist. Checklist 1* gives some of the items that might be included in such an analysis. The astute salesman can readily add his own categories.

Because of the high incidence of structural change in most companies, the salesman will find it increasingly difficult to have any customer or function or business in his pocket for very long. His sponsors can move up or be moved out at any time and be replaced by decision makers and influencers with different, even antagonistic personality profiles. Their loyalties are more likely to be directed to advancing their own careers and ideals of professional performance than to any salesman or supplier.

As his customers become more professional and their or-

* See pages 74 to 80 for checklists.

ganizations grow more complex and sophisticated, a consultative salesman must develop the ability to profile his customer organizations as fluently as he perceives the personalities of his customers themselves. Every organization will present two faces to him. One is the face of the apparent organization, which is represented by the "paper logic" of the organization chart and the semantics of business management as expressed in position descriptions, policy statements, and programmed activities. This is the face the consultative salesman must penetrate. He must get through to the real face of the organization which reveals its political power structure and the mix of pseudo-friendships, covert jealousies, uneasy alliances, and complex interpersonal roles which compose it.

If he is going to develop an ability to be organizationally perceptive, the salesman will need to profile six aspects of the decision-making process within each customer company where he hopes to consult: the organization's power structure, influence system, political system, value system, role system, and group system. Each of these aspects of an organization's decision-making mechanism will carry a different weight of importance for almost every company. In a small organization, one may rule. In larger companies a mix of several can be dominant. Some companies decide from the top down; others from the bottom up. Individual decisions must be sought in a manner separate from participative decisions. The information that goes into decisions differs widely from company to company, in terms of both quantity and richness. Criteria for decisions are as variable as responsibility for them.

PROFILING A CUSTOMER'S POWER STRUCTURE

Power is the ability to impose will. In a customer organization, the power a man has can be perceived by the number of options open to him and his ability to choose the one he wants. The more numerous the options and the freer the choice among them, the greater the power. Power is not what a person *has*. It is the resultant of his relationship and interaction with others.

Power in any organization is difficult to perceive. For one thing, it is fragmented. No one has it all; everyone has some; very few have none. Power is also limited. The more one man has, the less there is to go around. Furthermore, power is rarely delegated. It is generally grasped rather than awarded. A fourth fact about power is probably the most difficult to deal with. Power comes in several varieties. One kind can approve action and get things done. Another kind can veto action and keep things from getting done. A third kind can mediate between the other two.

Position power. Every title carries an electrical charge. Many titles, though, appear more highly charged than they really are. Sometimes titles are bestowed in place of power. A truly powerful decision maker is the consultative salesman's natural client. Together they can make plans that carry a high level of confidence about their translation into action. There are no other power wielders in an organization about whom a salesman can make that statement.

Expert power. Many a decision maker is merely authorizing the recommendations of those people in the organization that possess an expertise on which he is almost wholly dependent. They possess expert power·

Referent power. The most personal kind of power in an organization is the referent power possessed by influencers. These are men whose recommendations are esteemed enough to be listened to and incorporated into action by position power holders. Pinpointing influencers is one of the most important tasks confronting a consultative salesman. If he pinpoints wrong, he risks the loss of time, effort, and money. By pinpointing correctly, he can add a major lubricant to his selling relationship. There are four keystones to profiling a customer's power structure.

1. Identify the different kinds of clout in a customer organization. First, find out who has *power over*. They can compel others. Then find out who has *power to*. They can affect what is done. Finally, identify those who have *power in*. They can exert power in certain situations, but in others their power ceases or is quite limited. If the situation is right for them, they can often be the most helpful of all.

2. Correlate titles with actual power. A title may equal only paper power. Nor does a title give its holder all kinds of power.

3. Construct power charts for each key account. On them, identify all power holders and the type of power they carry. Map the power struggles that go on between them. Show the contending sides and their relative strengths. Show the no-man's land between the factions where it can be fatal to take a stand.

4. Apply the power chart against a background chart of the customer's formal organization. This will show where authority and power coincide and where each exists without the other. This discovery can be the salesman's most helpful interpersonal guide.

Checklist 2 gives some of the items that are of interest in analyzing the power structure of an organization. You can, of course, add others of your own.

PROFILING A CUSTOMER'S INFLUENCE SYSTEM

Just as power is grasped, influence is gained. Influence can sometimes be a form of personal power. But it is not always so. In every customer organization, some influencers are also decision makers. Other influencers make no decisions themselves but give a decision maker his dominant direction. An executive secretary may influence the purchase of typewriters and dictation equipment but the office manager makes the purchase. A hospital's purchasing agent signs the order but the hospital's medical staff makes the decisions. There are four keystones to profiling a customer's influence system.

1. Identify the members of a customer organization who appear to interact on a frequent and recurrent basis.

2. Make a note of which man initiates these interactions most often. Note also who the repetitive responders are.

3. Remember whose names, or what department names, are typically used by customers as representing checkpoints or referral stations to which the salesman's proposals must go for screening and recommendation before they can be acted on.

4. Construct an interaction grid composed of all identifiable influencers, together with the decision makers who refer to them or with whom they counsel. This will reveal at a glance the influential dynamics of a department, division, or company.

PROFILING A CUSTOMER'S POLITICAL SYSTEM

Customers are political animals. They use politics, which has been defined as the art of the possible, to govern themselves in a far more realistic manner than an organization chart can provide. The reason for this is found in the way a company's political system complements its organizational system. An organizational system allows its members to achieve corporate objectives. A political system allows them to reach their own personal objectives. When the two systems get out of kilter with each other, compromise must take place. Some form of domination or integration has to be worked out or discord will occur.

The consultative salesman must be both aware and wary of his customer organization's political system. His awareness will sensitize him to learning who among the politicians already hold office or who are quietly running for election. His wariness will help him remain a prudent observer and avoid taking sides. There are six keystones to profiling a customer's political system.

1. Identify the members of a customer organization who have organizational power. Next, identify those who have political power. Correlate the two groups. Mark for special attention the customers who have both kinds of power as well as those who have political power without equally important stature in their organizations.

2. Locate the in-group. At the same time, label each out-group.

3. Make note of common interests which have the potential ability of causing the in-group to join forces with an out-group. Also note the situations in which two or more out-groups would find a common cause.

4. Sketch out the circumstances in which an out-group could become the in-group and the in-group an out-group. List the probable effects of such a flip-flop on the selling climate.

5. Pay keen attention to the role of politics in setting budgets and determining promotions up the ladder of authority.

6. Construct a political maze showing the concentrations and interrelations between the organizational and political power

groups in each customer company. Label them in rank order from the most powerful down to the least.

PROFILING A CUSTOMER'S VALUE SYSTEM

Every customer company has its own value system. It places importance on certain principles and premises by assuming them to be more or less eternal truths. Values are rarely committed to writing. Instead, they are communicated informally from person to person. In this way, the salesman's customers come to know that they are their organization's kind of people and that therefore there is a right way to do things and other things just aren't done.

The consultative salesman must regard his customer's value system as a *code of ethics.* Whether or not he agrees with it or even approves of it, he must respect it. Since the value system of a customer organization sets its self-image, the salesman must correlate his own image with its most important aspects if he wants to be identified with them. A risk-taking, aggressive, innovative salesman probably cannot gain the confidence he needs to do business with a cautious, conservative organization which takes pride in maintaining a low profile inside and out.

There are three keystones to profiling a customer's value system. (1) Characterize the predominant values that an organization professes or exhibits. Note whether it stresses innovation or stability, the achievement of success or the avoidance of failure. (2) Evaluate the extent to which it practices decentralized profit-centering, functional or divisional autonomy, and the delegation of individual decision making as opposed to centralized committee rule. (3) Itemize what constitutes esteemed, tolerated, and forbidden behavior. Construct a value index of approved and disapproved styles. Attach an intensity factor to each one.

PROFILING A CUSTOMER'S ROLE SYSTEM

Roles are behavior styles. When a customer plays the role of being a customer, he acts out of a mixture of two converging forces. The first is his own self-perceived role in which he expresses his concept of what a customer does and how he does it. This concept is usually a synthesis of the conversational and action styles of several role models who have been the customer's managers or peers. The second is his role as others in the organization have let him know they perceive it. The perception that a customer holds a tough job often determines for him that he must act like a tough customer who gives salesmen a hard time. Checklist 3 provides some guidelines for analyzing the role adopted by your counterpart.

Much role playing is behind price resistance. So is status, which may be reflected by a role or exceeded by the way the role is played out. Role playing sometimes must be given deference which a salesman would ordinarily reserve for true status. There are four keystones to profiling a customer's role system.

1. Identify the roles each decision maker and influencer in a customer organization projects outward. Identify, too, the *role expectations* they have of you—how they expect you to act toward them. Correlate each role with the player's position, power, and values. Earmark the role-magnifiers for reassuring and ego-enhancing treatment.

2. Define the types of role conflict which decision makers and influencers seem to be having. Note the effects they have on salesman relations.

3. Note the members of a customer organization who use their power to impose defensive roles on their suppliers' salesmen.

4. Construct a customer role interface. Connect similar role players with each other. Isolate actual and potential role conflicts. Correlate roles with status in the organization.

PROFILING A CUSTOMER'S GROUP SYSTEM

In most decision-making situations that confront a consultative salesman, the decisive unit is not an individual but a group. A group is two or more people who interact in such a way as to provide "rewards" and "costs" for one another. The group may be a formal buying committee or screening committee or selection committee or it may be informal. Because individuals act in different ways when they are part of a group, the salesman must know the groupings in his customer organizations which can affect them and, as a result, also affect him.

In many instances, groups can reinforce an individual customer's decision. They can also negate it. Groups work through social pressure. They set their own norms, impose standards, reward and punish isolates and nonconformers, and can enforce attitude and behavior changes by their members.

Every group, whether formal or informal, has its own personality, customs, and unwritten laws. Each has its especially tender nerves and sensitivities. Groups find ways of relating to one another. They have their own internal pecking order and external status ranking. In many organizations the informal groups rule. The consultative salesman must be able to seek them out and penetrate their deliberations either personally or through the mediation of an internal influencer. In this way, he can participate in their decisions which will affect his relationship with the organization.

There are five keystones to profiling a customer's group system.

1. Identify the customer's major deciding groups, both formal and informal. Assign each group a rank order of pressure which it can exert on the others.

2. Specify the reactions which pressured groups use to withstand pressure or turn it around.

3. Make note of group leaders, especially those who lead both formal and informal groups at one and the same time.

4. Itemize and classify the decisions that come out of each kind of group. Understand the decision areas where formal and informal groups work in harmony and where they clash so that their decisions thwart each other or cancel each other out.

5. Construct a group chart showing each group, its key members, the kinds of decisions they make, whether each is formal or informal, and how they interrelate. Checklists 4 and 5 give some idea of how you might go about this.

PREPARING FOR PERCEPTIVE NEGOTIATION

Every sales relationship runs the risk of becoming the product of what can be called the *trained incapacities* of the salesman and his customer. Each of them may suffer, in greater or lesser degree, from an inability to perceive their sales situation from a point of view that is significantly different from past learning or experience. Most selling situations therefore yield to the persistent temptation to use yesterday's experience to give today's answers to tomorrow's problems.

The more a sales relationship regresses to a familiar pattern, the more likely it is that its participants will believe the situation to be manipulative for the salesman and defensive for the customer. The salesman then sees himself playing an aggressive, persuasive role that is intended to reduce the customer's options to resist. The customer, naturally, reacts defensively to preserve his options. He looks for outs and tries to keep them open. The salesman tries to close them one by one until purchase remains the sole avenue of escape. This is the *escape into purchase,* which has saved so many salesmen at one time or another in their careers but has alienated so many customers for all time.

In such a selling situation, the salesman's approach is on a me-versus-you basis with the customer. One and only one of them can win. In the consultative selling situation, however, both must win. Here the salesman's point of view must be a *we* orientation. His basis of operating must therefore be altered from aggressive action on his part to joint interaction with his customer. He must conduct himself in a consultant's role, which means he will be able to influence his customer's attitudes and eventual behavior because the customer himself comes to realize that the salesman's efforts are geared to the customer's best interests.

Persuasion has an undeniable place in achieving this result. But it is insufficient by itself. So are communication and motivation, or any of the traditional stereotypes of what makes customers buy. The consultative salesman must rely instead on the process of *negotiation* as the basis for his client relationships.

Negotiation is the act of bargaining to reach an agreed-upon objective. The negotiators—the consultative salesman and his customer—must see themselves and each other as equals if true negotiation is to take place. They will not be equal in the same ways, of course. The customer can still say no and nullify the salesman's best efforts. The salesman can withhold his best efforts and nullify the customer's attempt to achieve his objectives. But the essential area where equality must prevail is in their mutual respect, the sense each has of being a vital contributor to the fulfillment of their common needs. When this occurs, the most important ingredient of the consultative sales approach is in place: *Through the process of negotiation, the customer becomes transformed into a client.*

To become an effective negotiator with a key-account customer, the consultative salesman must put to work his analysis of three profiles he has created: his profile of the customer's personality, his profile of the customer's organization, and his profile of his own personality. Drawing on these analytical profiles, the salesman can prepare himself for the customer negotiations he will begin to undertake as his new way of life.

GETTING THE BIG PICTURES IN THE MIND

Salesmen and their customers do not really negotiate with each other. Their assumptions, attitudes, and perceptions of each other create the pictures in their minds, and it is these pictures in the mind that interact, not the salesman and customer. Unless the salesman can get at the big pictures in his customer's mind, he will generate more misunderstanding than understanding when he attempts to negotiate.

Several snapshotting questions lead to the development of the mental pictures that occur in the minds of both a salesman and his customer: How do I see myself in this relationship? How do I see him? How do I think he sees me? How do I think he should see me? How would I like him to see me? For each key customer, the consultative salesman should maintain a psychological "photo album" in which he can profile the major mental pictures that determine the negotiating base of his relationship. Checklist 6 gives a guide for keeping these "images" in focus.

GETTING OUT OF YOURSELF

To negotiate successfully, the salesman must practice getting out of himself and "getting into" his customer. This requires the application of eight practical principles of customer behavior.

1. Every customer is naturally concerned for the satisfaction of his own needs and interests.

2. Every customer will define what is real in his own terms, as he perceives and experiences it.

3. All customer behavior, however irrational it may appear, is purposeful and goal-directed. It is multimotivated. It is caused. It makes sense to the customer at the time he acts.

4. The only propositions a customer really understands are those he has experienced. The only courses of action he really supports are those in which he has participated.

5. A customer will do one of three things when he is faced with a new proposition: assimilate it if it is consistent with his own experience, distort it enough to make it fit his experience if it is somewhat inconsistent, or block it out completely or alter it radically to reduce its threat if it is totally new.

6. Different functionaries in a customer's organization think differently because they always tend to see things from their own perspective.

7. A customer's attitudes are often more motivating than his logic. But he will always defend his attitudes as being entirely logical.

8. The best vantage point for understanding a customer's behavior is within his internal frame of reference.

EMPATHY

Successful negotiation depends on the salesman's ability to act as a relationship builder who can think with his customer. This aptitude is called empathy. It has also been called the consultant's bridge to his customer, the communication pathway that enables two men to work with each other in commitment to a single common objective. Empathy also has a feeling component. Unlike sympathy, which suggests a *feeling for* someone else, empathy enables the consultative salesman to *feel with* his customer without becoming emotionally involved or blinded by the same emotional frame of reference. The key to empathy is not to try to become the other man. On the contrary, it is to be very much oneself but to act, think, and feel with the other man so that the two can combine their powers to solve one problem.

In order to become empathetic and cross the bridge into partnership with his customer, the salesman must commit himself to majoring in customer needs and sought for benefits as his principal preparation for perceptive negotiation.

CUSTOMER NEED-SEEKING

If the consultative salesman is to abandon any attempt to outwit his customer, or to manipulate him, he must find a new basis for doing business with him. This basis cannot be a contrived one, such as assuming that the customer really wants to buy and the salesman only has to make it possible by ruling out the alternatives. Nor does it encompass treating the customer as a simple responder to the salesman's stimulus. No customer is such a predictable animal that he can be expected to faithfully and forever react in the same way to the salesman's famous four steps of attracting attention, arousing interest, creating desire, and obtaining action.

The consultative salesman can negotiate with his customer only on the basis of seeking out his needs and then helping him to satisfy them. This process begins with the shared development of customer needs. It then moves on to a shared awareness of customer needs, when both the salesman and his customer perceive the same needs with equal clarity. Finally, through joint need fulfillment, the salesman can accomplish his profit improvement objectives in the course of helping his customer realize his own objectives.

The consultative salesman must therefore be first and foremost a developer of customer needs. These are his raw materials. Negotiation is the process by which raw needs are refined, their key ingredients are extracted, and the solutions that are always within them are distilled and packaged as profit improvement projects.

Needs are not developed easily because they are not revealed freely. A customer's needs are among his most proprietary possessions. From a competitive perspective, it is more helpful in analyzing a rival company's potential threat to know what its needs are than to know what its accomplishments have been. Its needs are the basis of its objectives, and objectives are the most precious of all industrial intelligence. After all, the historical situation that underlies a business is known to all. The strategies by which a business attempts to reach its planned objectives become public information as soon as they are executed. But the objectives themselves are always zealously guarded because they and they alone contain the secrets of the future of the business.

For this reason, it has been said that you don't learn needs—you earn the *right* to learn them. Because needs are so confidentially held, the consultative salesman will rarely be able to learn them swiftly or all at once. There are some needs he will never be able to discover in their most exacting, precise sense. To the extent that he can be perceived as more of a consultant than a salesman, however, he can help create the climate of confidence in which an interchange of need revelation and fulfillment can take place. Without them, there can never be a significant degree of confidence in a relationship. Where need revelation and fulfillment are not shared—where it becomes apparent to both the consultative salesman and his customer that the needs of only one of them are being met—the relationship will be inherently unstable and will not endure. Two people cannot long sustain a voluntary relationship that benefits only one of them.

SALESMAN–CUSTOMER MOTIVATION SETS

In the course of having his needs developed through negotiation, the customer will probably have his first experience in being a *client*. From it, he will derive his first impressions of the salesman's professional skills. This impression forms the basis for respect. From the same experience, the customer also derives his first impressions of the salesman's intellectual honesty. This impression forms the basis for confidence. To initiate the customer into clienthood, the salesman must become aware of a client's motivations and how they differ from his own in his role as a relationship-building consultant.

The salesman's motivation set. Salesmen have traditionally been taught to motivate others. Rarely have they been educated to motivate themselves or to analyze their own motivations. What makes a customer tick is vital sales intelligence. But what makes the salesman himself tick is vital self-intelligence. Without it, the salesman can easily become his own worst enemy. It will not be his customer's resistance that will defeat him; it will be his own deficiencies.

The salesman's motivation set can be thought of as being composed of three aspects. Each aspect represents a certain type of income that the salesman wants to receive: *money income; psychic income,* representing such rewards as power, prestige, and promotion; and what can be summarized as *self-actualization income,* including expressions of self-fulfillment, competence, and the realization of the salesman's talent potential through his career.

These three aspects of motivation are present in every salesman's motivation set. Yet they vary widely in proportion from one salesman to another. To negotiate effectively, a consultative salesman's motivation set must be proportioned along the lines of Figure 2.7. The power aspect of a consultant's income must necessarily be small. Although he may enjoy great prestige, he will always be required to work through his customer to accomplish his purposes. He can help a customer achieve power and promotion and thereby share vicariously in these income sources. But he will often work unheralded, and it will be the rule rather than the exception to find himself largely anonymous among the acknowledged contributors to his customer's accomplishments.

A consultative salesman must, on the other hand, have an unusually large amount of self-actualization in his motivation set. This aspect is the key to his consultancy. He must have, and be driven by, a great need to realize his own fullest growth and development as a salesman. He must want to utilize all of himself in his customer's behalf, engaging his full system of talents and skills and expressing his widest range of knowledge. He must need to translate these qualities into unique profit projects that could have come from him alone and that have a form and content bearing the unmistakable imprint of his personal style.

The customer's motivation set. In his role as a consultative salesman's customer, a man must emphasize certain aspects of his motivation set. These aspects, more than any others, determine how he will move, if at all, in approaching or avoiding the salesman's profit improvement recommendations and how swift, vigorous, and committed his movement will be.

In Figure 2.8 three aspects of a customer's motivation set

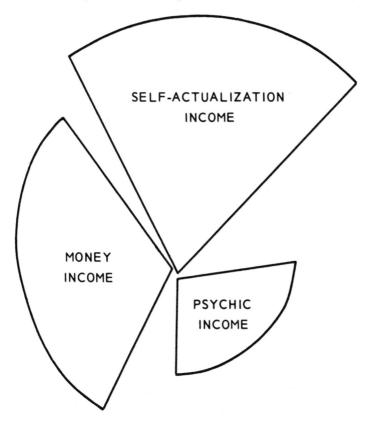

Figure 2.7   The salesman's motivation set.

are illustrated in typical proportion to each other. They contrast interestingly with the proportions shown in Figure 2.8 for the same three aspects of the consultative salesman's motivation set. The major difference lies in the relative significance of self-actualization income and psychic income. For the consultative salesman, self-actualization must always take precedence over the psychic rewards of power, prestige, and promotion. For his customer, however, the salesman should assume that power and promotion—which represent realizable objectives for a customer—can supersede self-fulfillment. By acting as though this were true in most of his negotiations, the salesman will be able to keep his customer's perspective in mind. He will also be able to visualize himself fairly accurately in the way his customer will be positioning him: as a man who can help the customer achieve increased power income within his company and in the same process maximize his money income as well.

The consultative salesman must achieve harmony in his relationships by integrating his motivation set with that of his customer. The initiative must be his. It is his task to perceive himself,

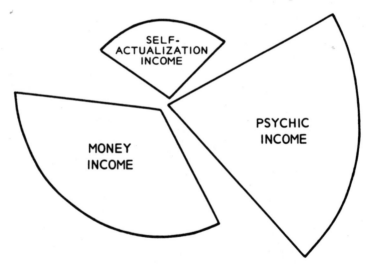

Figure 2.8   The customer's motivation set.

first of all, in the power-accelerator role that his customer perceives for him. Second, the salesman must devote his own self-actualization motives to his customer's best interests. And third, the salesman must adopt a posture of empathy with his customer so that the motivation sets of the two men can operate smoothly as one.

INTERACTING WITH THE SIX PEOPLE IN EVERY TWO

As the consultative salesman and his customer get into a relationship with each other, it only seems as though just the two of them are involved. In reality, as many as six "people" may be interacting. Within each of them, a parent aspect, an adult aspect, and a child aspect may be contained. When the salesman and his customer negotiate with each other, their parent aspects—or one parent aspect and one child aspect—may actually make the transactions.

The *parent* is the superior, self-righteous, all-knowing, sometimes patronizing and condescending but basically dictatorial aspect of personality. The *child* is the personality aspect that has never grown up. He is demanding of special favors and considerations, dependent on the approval of others, complaining when it is withheld, and often bragging endlessly about it when it has been received. The *adult* is the mediator. This role is to prevent the personality from being dominated by the aspect of either the parent or the child. The adult is the most rational of the three. While the parent and child are willing to sacrifice reality to satisfy short-term feelings, the adult sacrifices feelings for the sake of more enduring satisfactions.

THE HARRIS APPROACH

How OK the salesman and his customer are, and how OK they perceive themselves and each other to be, can have a significant influence on how effectively they can negotiate. Dr. Thomas A. Harris has defined four basic attitudes that may accelerate or negate the salesman's ability to be a successful negotiator.[4]

[4] Thomas A. Harris, *I'm OK—You're OK: A Practical Guide to Transactional Analysis* (New York: Harper & Row, 1967, 1968, 1969).

I'm not OK—you're OK. A salesman with this attitude comes into the negotiation process in an inferior position. He perceives his customer as superior. He may react by giving away more than he could bargain for in an attempt to curry the customer's favor. Or he may attempt to attract a compensating amount of attention to himself so as to even up the interpersonal balance. In doing so, he may create irritation and resentment. As yet another recourse, the salesman may avoid interacting with certain customers and withdraw completely from calling on them.

I'm not OK—you're not OK. A salesman who holds this attitude is prejudicing his ability to negotiate before he begins. If he finds a customer with the same attitude, the two of them may become unaware cooperators in a negotiation process whose failure is assured.

I'm OK—you're not OK. A salesman with this attitude bears the greatest liability as a negotiator. He perceives himself as the good guy; the customer is the bad guy. When anything goes wrong, the salesman naturally blames the customer. A customer who has this attitude will often surround himself with yes-men who will screen out the salesman's direct contact with his customer.

I'm OK—you're OK. A salesman with this attitude can negotiate on an adult-to-adult basis. He and his customer can do business with each other openly and cooperatively on a mutually beneficial basis. They can forsake the Berne-like games which people play when the children or parents in them are the negotiators.

The Harris approach to negotiation suggests four guidelines for the consultative salesman to follow as he prepares to negotiate with his customer.

1. Keep your parent and child selves under control. Don't let them contaminate your adult self.
2. Be sensitive to the customer's parent and child selves. Your adult self can cope with them if you are aware that they are dominant. Look for negativism, pettiness, and aggressiveness to perceive the customer's child self. His parent self will appear in the form of absolute judgments and rigid points of view. Neither the customer's parent self nor his child self can be negotiated with solely on the basis of logic.

3. Avoid complementary transactions. Don't reinforce the customer's child or parent self with your own. Only adult-to-adult transactions are generally productive.
4. Adopt a supplementary role when necessary. A dependent customer whose child aspect is uppermost may require reassurance by the salesman's adult self.
5. Remember that you have a so-called life-script comprising your past psychological history. So, too, does the customer, to the extent that you can (a) be aware of each, and (b) prevent them from clashing.

THE JOHARI WINDOW ON SELF-AWARENESS

If true negotiation is to take place, the salesman and his customer have a similar task: to make the public area of their interaction as large as possible. Figure 2.9 follows the approach

SALESMAN

	Known	*Unknown*
Known	Public	Blind
Unknown	Hidden	Unknown

(CUSTOMER, with *Known* and *Unknown* row labels)

Figure 2.9   The Johari window.

of the so-called Johari "window,"[5] which divides a salesman's and customer's life awareness into four major sectors. The public sector includes the knowledge each possesses about the other's personality. The unknown area represents personality aspects neither is cognizant of. The blind sector consists of the salesman's personality

---

[5] Joseph Luft, *Group Processes: An Introduction to Group Dynamics* (Palo Alto, Calif.: National Press, 1963). *See also,* Robert T. Golembiewski and Arthur Blumberg, eds., *Sensitivity Training and the Laboratory Approach* (Itasca, Ill.: F. E. Peacock Publishers, 1970).

characteristics which the customer sees but the salesman himself is blind to. Finally, the hidden sector contains aspects of the salesman's personality which he does not reveal to the customer. The same ideas, of course, apply to the customer.

Only by enlarging the public sector of their Johari window and reducing the unknown, hidden, and blind sectors to a minimum can a salesman and his customer negotiate.

Disclosure and feedback are the two most useful strategies for opening up the public area of their window. When the salesman reveals his authentic self, he permits his customer to feel comfortable with him. He also puts the customer under subtle pressure to respond in kind. This creates the reciprocity and reinforcement which are vital to negotiation. Every time the salesman and his customer trade off feedback freely and openly, they reinforce the team basis of the consultative relationship.

These guidelines about self-disclosure and feedback can be helpful to the salesman preparing for negotiation.[6]

How much you disclose and feed back is important. Too little self-disclosure denies appropriate clues. It creates a climate of no-confidence in which each negotiator may become defensive and suspicious of the other's motives. On the other hand, overdoing disclosure creates uneasiness, embarrassment, and the suspicion that the relationship may be too good to be true.

When you disclose and feed back is also an important consideration. Too early disclosure often appears as too much too soon. It comes through as insincere. Or it may be interpreted as manipulative, an inducement to the other person to reveal aspects of himself which he would prefer to withhold. Late disclosure and feedback may also be ineffective, since it leads to the inference that what is being done is done reluctantly or only under pressure.

What is revealed is a third major consideration. The content of the salesman's self-disclosure should take into account the needs and concerns of his customer and the probable supportive effect of his revelations on the course of their relationship. Only feedback which strengthens and reinforces their work together should be emphasized. This means it must be relevant in content and constructive in intent.

[6] *Ibid.*

How the salesman positions his inquiries to draw out the customer and how he presents his own revelations are vital. He must avoid frontal assaults which will arouse his customer's defenses or cause him to withdraw and adopt a protective "distancing behavior." Indirect attempts are best in smoking out highly sensitive information. But they should not be so obviously indirect that they can be seen through in a way that makes them seem to be trick questions or loaded ones.

THE FOUR SALESMAN–CUSTOMER IMAGES

Before the consultative salesman can enter into personal negotiation with his customer, he must clarify several images in his own mind. Each of these images is in the form of a mental picture, a photograph not of people but of their perceptions. The interaction that occurs between the salesman and his customer will be largely determined by these perceptions. In fact, as Figure 2.10 suggests, it will occur between the perceived images far more often than between the salesman and his customer themselves.

The salesman's self-image. The salesman must learn to see

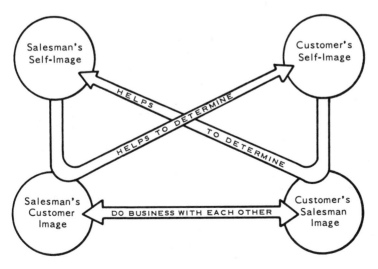

Figure 2.10 Salesman–customer images.

himself as an integrator. He must understand that his central objective is to help the customer achieve his own objectives. He must therefore dedicate himself to play a supportive role that integrates their dual needs rather than a competitive one.

The salesman's customer image. The salesman's customer image will generally be composed of three characteristics. One is the salesman's perceptions of his customer. A second image characteristic will be the salesman's fears or hopes about his customer. The third image characteristic will be the salesman's beliefs about why his customer thinks what he thinks, says what he says, and does what he does.

The customer's self-image. Although the consultative salesman can affect the first two images—his own self-image and his image of the customer—the third image is almost entirely beyond his control. The customer's self-image, whether it is accurate or biased, is a "given" with which the salesman will have to deal. No matter how mistaken he perceives it to be, the salesman will have to accept it as representing reality.

The customer's salesman image. The customer's image of the consultative salesman is the corollary of the salesman's image of his customer. These are the two images that "do business" with each other. The customer goes about constructing his image of the salesman in exactly the same way the salesman gathers his perceptions of the customer. A union of fact and fancy, rationality and irrationality, is always involved. Yet the salesman has a continuing opportunity to influence his customer's image of him by making sure that everything he says and does reflects the salesman's objective of representing an added value. If the salesman can come to be regarded as an achievement aid, an accomplishment enhancer, and a profit assurer, he will have created the optimal image for consultative negotiation.

PERCEPTIVE NEGOTIATION STRATEGIES

Negotiation does not take place when a salesman and his customer simply sit down and say, "Let's negotiate." Negotiation requires that seemingly divergent points of view become compatible. Each negotiator must feel he has won something, as indeed he has. The payoff will be different for the salesman and his customer. Nonetheless, it will be mutually rewarding. Both men can be satisfied that their objectives have been met and their needs fulfilled. Neither should regret the other's fulfillment because it has not been made at his expense. This is why negotiation allows both parties to come out ahead.

Negotiation's first law is that both sides win. Unlike Lombardi's first law, which says that only one side wins, negotiation allows the salesman and his customer to secure what each holds to be principally important. Consultative negotiation is earmarked by five characteristics.

1. It begins and ends with equals. The equality of the two negotiators comes from the fact that each has a similar need for the other man to achieve his objectives. Otherwise, each will remain incomplete and ineffective.

2. It seeks to integrate different points of view so that neither negotiator is forced to yield anything that is really important to him. Persuasion, accommodation, and compromise can contain the seeds of future disagreement and even conflict. But integration has the potential for building a stable relationship free of one-upmanship or waiting out a chance to get even.

3. It takes place only in a climate of confidence. The mutual respect which must underlie negotiation has two foundations. One is the confidence each negotiator has that his own self-interest will be served. The second is his confidence that the other man's self-interest is open and fully disclosed to him, that he does not have to be on the lookout for hidden motivations or latent surprises. This helps him believe that his needs will be served in a way that will leave behind no recriminations.

4. It achieves a "coincidence of opposites." Under negotiation, the traditional you-and-me attitude of salesman and customer becomes *we*. The success of the negotiation, as opposed to the success of one of the negotiators, emerges as the overriding objective.

5. It is deeply concerned with need awareness, need identification, need clarification, and need serving by each negotiator

in the interest of the other. The purpose of emphasizing needs in this manner is to arrive at a solution by consensus. In this respect, negotiation follows the principle that says: Never use another person merely as a means to your purposes; never allow yourself to be used as a means to the purposes of another.

These characteristics of negotiation all stress collaboration, cooperation, and coordination between salesman and customer. In these ways the negotiation process is distinguished from the alternative strategies of persuasion, accommodation, and compromise.

NEGOTIATION VERSUS PERSUASION

Persuasion differs from negotiation because it subtly imposes the salesman's will on the customer. It tries to win the customer over, counteract his objections, and bring him around to the salesman's point of view. At best, persuasion can achieve only a temporary or reluctant submission rather than deep-seated lasting agreement. Once persuaded rarely means always persuaded.

When a salesman uses persuasion as his habitual bargaining strategy, it leaves the customer with the inference that the salesman knows what is best for him. If the customer can also believe that the salesman has his best interests at heart, persuasion may be acceptable. But this is rarely the case. More than likely, the customer will become defensive under repeated persuasion. A boomerang effect may occur which can make the salesman's persuasion counterproductive. The customer may then exert one or more forms of defensive persuasion against the salesman. The three major types of protective defenses and some of the behaviors that result for them are shown in Figure 2.11.

NEGOTIATION VERSUS ACCOMMODATION

Accommodation differs from negotiation because it is unilateral, not reciprocal. One man is positioned as superior to the other. The inferior man is expected to accommodate his needs to those of his superior, usually the customer.

While negotiation allows for mutual accommodation, it also channels the salesman's adaptations to it within four boundaries: the salesman's own convictions, his company's poli-

Figure 2.11   Protective defense mechanisms.

TYPE OF PROTECTIVE DEFENSE	ILLUSTRATION
SELF-DECEPTIVE MECHANISMS	
Attention-getting and egocentricity	The customer who goes out of his way to be in the limelight or who constantly talks about himself, his expertise, or his shrewdness in order to impress the salesman.
Compensation	The customer who has gone as far as he can go in his company and finds substitute satisfaction in acting as its resident expert.
Identification	The customer who constantly reminds the salesman that he is dealing with a prestigious firm simply because his own self-esteem comes mostly from his association with an industry leader.
Rationalization	
Sour grapes	The customer who says a proposed system is no good for his company when the real reason is that he does not understand it.
Sweet lemon	The customer who turns down a salesman with the comment, "What you propose may be better for some other company but we prefer what we're using now," when the truth is that he knows the proposed product is superior but fears he would be unable to get consent to buy it.

Figure 2.11   (continued)

TYPE OF PROTECTIVE DEFENSE	ILLUSTRATION
Sympathy-seeking	The customer who is always looking for a shoulder to cry on, saying "Between you and my boss, I'm always caught in the middle. I'm the fall guy."
Projection	The customer who complains to the salesman that everything wrong is the salesman's fault or who accuses the salesman of stubbornness and inflexibility when he himself is really the hard-headed one.
WITHDRAWAL MECHANISMS	
Denial	The customer who refuses to admit change by remarking, "These new-fangled ways of doing things are a flash in the pan. I'm from the old school. The old ways are the best ways."
Apathy	The customer who says, "Why rock the boat? Let's not make waves."
Escape	The customer who is always "busy," "tied up," or "in conference" when the salesman calls.
Forgetting	The customer who says to the salesman, "Gosh, I forgot to look into that. I'll get to it next time." But next time never comes.

Figure 2.11   (continued)

TYPE OF PROTECTIVE DEFENSE	ILLUSTRATION
Sickness	The customer who habitually misses appointments with the salesman because he gets sick with "convenience virus."
Regression	The customer who has tantrums because the salesman cannot let him have his own way.
AGGRESSIVE MECHANISMS	
Scapegoating	The customer who abuses the salesman because he feels the salesman is vulnerable and must sit there and take it.
Nagging	The customer who goes out of his way to make the salesman's life miserable by constant carping and complaining.
Domineering	The customer who is overbearing and insists the salesman do things his way and cater to his whims.
Negativism	The customer who seems to enjoy being picky and objects to even the most reasonable request or the most rational presentation.
Hostility	The customer who gives the salesman a hard time by making sarcastic or demeaning remarks.

cies and practices, the images they have created in the mind of his customer, and the need the salesman has to maximize the benefits his customer can obtain from dealing with him. Within these boundaries, the salesman can be accommodating to his customer without sacrificing either his personal identity or his professional integrity.

NEGOTIATION VERSUS COMPROMISE

Compromise differs from negotiation because it trades off some degree of give for an agreeable amount of take. It generally results in solutions that are acceptable but not satisfying to either of the two compromisers. Each regrets sacrificing something that he really wanted to retain or achieve. Often enough, both parties come away from a compromise feeling they have been cheated.

In every compromise, it is clear going in that both parties will probably have to give up something. The emphasis is on what will be lost, not gained. This expectation can breed suspicion and distrust. The compromisers become opponents, each playing a defensive game so that the other will be certain to sustain the greater loss. Because this hidden agenda dominates compromise, second guessing defeats openness and can cause excessive investment in time and energy. At the end of a compromise, instead of being replenished, compromisers are often exhausted. Since each has been forced to exaggerate his self-centeredness by making demands on the other, shared growth has been thwarted and rigid stands rather than flexibility have been encouraged.

NEGOTIATION PRINCIPLES

The principles of negotiation are essentially the elements of effective customer relations. Seven principles are the most important for the salesman to remember and put into practice.

1. Have respect for the customer. Earn his respect for you. Be yourself so he can know the proper "you" to have respect for. Avoid trying to dominate the relationship so that both of you can value it equally.

2. Act like a consultant. This means substituting a teach-

ing role for sales aggressiveness. The first thing to teach the customer is how to become a client. This means replacing his traditional customer defensiveness with a partnership approach that makes each profit improvement project a true joint venture.

3. Be open, intellectually accessible, and authentic. Disclose yourself and your motives to your customer. Start out by frankly and unashamedly admitting your self-interest in every transaction. Lay it on the line. In turn, allow the customer to reciprocate.

4. Before anything else, set objectives agreeable to both. Once the ends are accepted, the strategic means can be worked out. Spell out clearly how achievement of the objectives will benefit each of you.

5. Be empathetic about the customer's needs. Feel the situation from his perspective. Play it back to him as you feel it so he can validate your assumptions. Validation is the first step toward the successive agreements that must occur in a successful negotiation.

6. Communicate in a way that advances the relationship by adding new insights, additional revelations, and reinforcing feedback. Avoid communication that obscures. Discuss rather than debate.

7. Acknowledge the customer's need for his defense mechanisms. Don't try to beat your way through them or beat them down. Create a relationship with him that will make many of his accustomed defenses unnecessary.

NEGOTIATION STRATEGIES

When the consultative salesman gets down to specific cases in applying the principles of negotiation, he will find that each customer and each situation exert their own individual constraints on how far and how fast he can move. To help him, he should have a repertoire of negotiation strategies. He will always prefer to use the cooperative strategies, but his customers will not always accommodate him. He will therefore have to accommodate them in many cases.

Aggressively negotiating customers will often require the

salesman to be defensive or assertive. Unless he can deal with these situations, a salesman cannot sell consultatively. Certainly he will not be able to alter the personality or character of his customers. Since he cannot change them or ignore them, he must learn to cope with them. No matter what resistances he encounters, he will have to function professionally even when faced with customers who would depersonalize him, who enjoy manipulating him, who are seemingly immune to his influence, who prefer to keep their relationship with him ambiguous rather than secure, and who keep testing his limits and push him as far as he will let them go.

Cooperative strategies

Make the customer an ally. Seek to help the customer and let him know it. Use your complete array of company resources to create and widen areas of shared new learning between the two of you.

Put your cards on the table. Make it clear exactly what you can and cannot expect to accomplish. Make sure your expectations are the same since each of you will evaluate the relationship's success on how well they are met.

Be patient. Cultivate the ground, plant seeds of information and recommendation, and water them regularly. To attempt to harvest too soon may set the crop back by years. Offer service long before an order can be expected.

Disagree when necessary, but do so in the form of playing devil's advocate. This enables you to point out alternatives, project dire consequences, or tactfully indicate better ways of achieving objectives without directly confronting the customer's points of view.

Build on the customer's real strengths. Help him optimize what he already has going for him. Supplement his weaknesses. Make him *become* good, not just *look* good. Since opportunity equals need plus capability, contribute your capability to the customer's need.

Run behind your blockers. Develop influencers inside the customer's organization who can block out opposition for you.

Make time to make friends with the customer's subordinates, his associates, even his superiors.

Show extra effort. Perform at a level that the customer can perceive as being clearly above and beyond the routine sales call. This is especially important when the customer has a severe problem. Help him make lemonade out of his lemon.

Accommodative strategies

Yield diagonally. If a customer is insistent and you must accede to him or lose the sale, yield one or more slices of the item rather than nothing or everything. Practice slow, limited withdrawal. Often, enough can be saved this way to justify the effort.

Turn the other cheek. If you and your customer are both aware that the customer is at fault in a situation, accept part of the blame so that he can save face. This will help him appreciate one of the principal benefits of partnership with you.

Learn when to leave well enough alone. Forsake the goal of an ideal solution to every problem. There are times when the best policy is to take what the defense gives you.

Bide your time. It is often necessary to "go in the customer's door, though you fully intend to come out a door that is compatible to both of you." This may take time. At the opportune moment, retake the initiative. In negotiation, patience is still a virtue.

Defensive strategies

Prevent showdowns. If a customer initiates a confrontation, avoid allowing either of you to achieve a victory. If possible, avoid the battle entirely. In a situation that is going from bad to worse, it is sometimes wise to create a confrontation on your own terms. Position it as a shared learning experience, though, and not a war.

Stand pat. Take a firm stand in the face of unreasonable demands. Don't boast about it. Define your position in reasonable terms. Frequently this is sufficient, especially with a customer who is testing the salesman's boundaries to see how far he can be manipulated.

Get lost. If negotiation seems inopportune, try again another day. Adopt a low profile until the coast is clear. Come back when things are getting better after having been as bad as they can be.

Destroy a straw man. Give the customer a chance to work off aggression and win something by creating an unimportant side issue that looks real but is made of straw.

Run the end. Outflank a problem customer. Make allies with other people in his company. Use the buddy system with the customer as much as possible to avoid alienation. But if you have to run alone, do so cautiously and as openly as possible.

Counterattack. Keep a few strategic options open for boomeranging back an unjustified allegation or assault on your position. Expose just enough of this strategy to cause a diversion. That may be all you need to do. This is sometimes called the "yes, but" strategy.

Reverse your field. Take a different tack. Become a moving target by taking several different tacks. Keep the situation unbalanced until it settles out.

Make a tossed salad. Introduce new information periodically into the negotiation. Focus the discussion on the new information and away from the hot issues. This helps buy time.

Keep sawing wood. Stick to your plan and ignore as much as possible the customer's attitudes and counterproductive activities in the negotiation.

Be up for adoption. Induce the customer to join your side. Find a strong shared need such as helping him gain acceptance for your plans upstairs so that both of you can look good.

Assertive strategies

Come in high. Set initially high objectives and make high demands. After the trade-off you may end up with a greater payoff. By coming in high, you can unsettle the customer. By taking advantage of the room you have for compromise, you can help settle him again.

Trump his ace. Let him seem able to go all the way. Then trip him at the goal line with an attractive counterproposal.

Develop momentum. Take initiative right from the start by setting the objectives and moving firmly toward them. Force issues. Keep the pressure on. Once you grab a bull by the horns, don't let go.

Surprise him. Keep the customer off balance. Make him play "catch up." Use your information resources to stay one step ahead of the negotiation and pick his defenses to pieces.

Acquire a sword or a shield. Find a third party who favors your point of view and use him as a shield. Or find a third party who is depending on the customer's success for the achievement of his own objectives and will act as a sword on your behalf.

Carry a big stick. If your boundaries are ignored or exceeded, threaten to withdraw a vital service or take an appeal upstairs. You can usually do this only once in a relationship.

ROAD MAPPING A COOPERATIVE NEGOTIATION

Cooperative negotiation is the only true consultative strategy. In the rough-and-tumble real world of dealing with his customer under a variety of situations, the salesman can help himself by making a road map of how far he can go in giving and taking. The first area is the salesman's personal code or behavior, his need to be respected, the policies and procedures of his company, and his need to build a stable relationship with his customer; these form the boundaries for his negotiation strategy. Within these boundaries, the salesman should enter his *musts* and *intolerables.* These are his areas of no-compromise. He should know what they are before every major negotiation. Any course of action that contains even one of his intolerables must be rejected. On the other hand, any course of action he adopts will have to contain all of his musts to be acceptable.

Since the musts and intolerables impose severe constraints on the negotiation process, the salesman should keep them minimal. They are his hard core. He should leave as much room as possible around the core for give and take. Once his core is touched, the negotiation has reached a crisis. When both the salesman's core and his customer's core come into contact with each other, impasse occurs.

The second area to be mapped is the salesman's freedom of movement, in which the salesman can adjust, adapt, and accommodate his customer's needs. There are two categories of accommodations, those that are desirable and others that are undesirable. The salesman's objective as a negotiator should be to obtain as many of the desirable accommodations as possible and to accept few of the undesirable ones. In this way, the interpersonal basis of his business planning will be favorably disposed to success.

Checklist I
THE ORGANIZATION'S MAJOR TRAITS

Characteristic		Comments
Climate:		
Autocratic	_____	_____
Paternalistic	_____	_____
Bureaucratic	_____	_____
Democratic	_____	_____
Decision Makers:		
Improvers-innovators	_____	_____
Maintainers-"storekeepers"	_____	_____
Failure avoiders	_____	_____
MBO oriented	_____	_____
Tradition-routine bound	_____	_____
Self-Image:		
Risk-taking, creative	_____	_____
Industry leader	_____	_____
Conservative-traditional	_____	_____
Maturely sophisticated	_____	_____

Characteristic	Comments
Tempo:	
Fast-paced	_____ _____
Impulsive, erratic	_____ _____
Planful, deliberate	_____ _____
Slow-moving, change-resistant	_____ _____
Communication Patterns:	
Free and open	_____ _____
Defensive, secretive	_____ _____
Guarded, formal, "polite"	_____ _____
Downward-"imperative"	_____ _____
Decision-Making Process:	
One-man	_____ _____
Top in-group	_____ _____
Specialist group	_____ _____
Collaborative, participative	_____ _____
Company Personality:	
Task oriented	_____ _____
Improvement oriented	_____ _____
Status quo oriented	_____ _____
Conflicted, exploitive	_____ _____
Mutually suspicious	_____ _____
Mutually cooperative	_____ _____
Tone of Key Personnel:	
Conforming, apathetic	_____ _____
Mutually distrustful	_____ _____
Dependent, fearful	_____ _____
Achieving, success-seeking	_____ _____
Self-aggrandising	_____ _____

Checklist 2

ANALYZING THE ORGANIZATIONAL POWER STRUCTURE

Kind of power	Power holder(s)	Source of power	How exercised?
Power to do:			
Power over:			
Reward and punishment power:			
Personal and social power: Ability to influence decision makers			
Expert power:			
Power "brokers":			

Checklist 3
ANALYZING THE CUSTOMER'S ROLE ADOPTION

Role Adopted	Self-Imposed	Company Required
Partner in problem definition and solution	_____	_____
Shrewd bargainer	_____	_____
Obstacle builder	_____	_____
Fault-finding critic	_____	_____
Collaborative negotiator	_____	_____
Exploiting maneuverer	_____	_____
Decision maker	_____	_____
Decision recommender	_____	_____
Forceful initiator	_____	_____
Cooperative follower	_____	_____
Spokesman for company needs	_____	_____
Spokesman for self-centered wants	_____	_____
Help seeker	_____	_____
Help provider	_____	_____
Answer seeker	_____	_____
Answer provider	_____	_____
Aggressive attacker	_____	_____
Defensive "counter puncher"	_____	_____
Salesman supporter	_____	_____
Constructive participant	_____	_____
Pleader for special exceptions	_____	_____

Checklist 4
ANALYZING THE GROUP INTERACTION

Kind of Group	Comments

Decision-Making Groups:

Which groups make what
kinds of decisions? _____

Which decisions are delegated
to which groups? _____

By what process does each
group arrive at a decision? _____

By what criteria are
.decisions made? _____

Information-Providing Groups:

Kinds of information provided
by each _____

How does each group make
its influence felt? _____

Interacting Groups:

Which groups usually cause other
groups to respond to them _____

Which groups are usually the
responders? _____

Which groups interact frequently? _____

Which groups interact infrequently? _____

Which groups interact cooperatively? _____

Which groups interact antagonistically? _____

Which are in-groups with power? _____

Which are out-groups without power? _____

Which groups are cohesive and work
harmoniously together? _____

Which groups are internally torn
with dissention? _____

Checklist 5
ANALYZING THE INTERACTION PATTERN
WITHIN A GROUP

Within Each Key Group, Identify Those Who:	*Comments*
Possess expert power	
Have referent power and influence with the group	
Have the "ear" of superiors	
Exert influence in other departments	
Are listened to by the members of the group	
Usually band together	
Generally are opposed to each other	
Serve as spokesmen for the group's ideas and feelings	
Usually adopt leadership roles	
Generally adopt followership roles	
Often come up with good ideas	
Frequently come up with effective practical strategies for getting things done	
Try to manipulate the group	
Go their own way and "listen to their own drummer"	
Are respected by other group members	
Usually serve as mediators and conciliators of opposing views	
Usually cause trouble and friction within the group	
Have a reputation for knowing what is going on or will take place	
Know how to work within the system, avoiding the rocks and shoals	

Checklist 6
ANALYZING THE IMAGE INTERACTION PATTERN

I	My Counterpart
How I see myself in this relationship	How he sees himself in this relationship
How I see him	How he sees me
How I think he sees me	How he thinks I see him
How I feel he should see me	How he feels I should see him
How I would like him to see me	How he would like me to see him
How I feel I ought to treat him	How he feels he ought to treat me
How I would like him to treat me	How he would like me to treat him
How I think he would like me to treat him	How he thinks I would like him to treat me

3 / Business Planning Strategies

THE CLIMATE OF CONFIDENCE is the salesman's context for consultative selling. The salesman must use the climate to grow his plans to help improve customer profit.

Customer profit plans are the working tools of a consultative relationship. They are the salesman's products, since it is the benefits contained in his plans for profit improvement which the customer will be asked to buy rather than the physical products that are a part of their strategies. Profit improvement plans are the consultative salesman's stock in trade. Their use will help replace the customer's traditional question, "What do you want to sell me today?" with the more consultative inquiry, "How much profit do you want to improve for me?"

The consultative salesman is a practitioner of five business planning strategies. He must be able to define his customer's market and understand its needs. Then he must be able to define the customer's business as a response to market needs. Third, he will have to be able to position his customer's products and services in terms of their profit improvement potential so that he can blueprint his prime selling opportunities. Fourth, he will have to integrate this knowledge of customer markets, business, and products into an information bank which he will draw upon to execute his fifth strategy, the creation of his portfolio of profit improvement miniplans.

The consultative salesman's planning contribution is central to his role. Without it, he falls back to being a traditional product salesman. In that case, he will be selling periodic batches of cataloged items to his customers on their demand-feeding schedule and under price and delivery pressures often generated by their own lack of planning or by competitive blue-sky promises. Consultative selling cannot guarantee the elimination of pitfalls in doing business with customers who do not plan or who make bad plans. But selling consultatively reduces many of the financial, operational, and emotional hazards that occur when one poorly planned company does business with another. At the same time, it forces customer decision making about the choice of suppliers onto personal service grounds where preemption is possible and away from product or pricing comparisons where preemption has become rare.

If the salesman and his company's products and services do not become integral parts of his customer's business plans, he will be unable to sell as a consultant. He will enjoy no partnership and none of the benefits of partnership that can accrue to his customers, his company, and himself from consultative selling.

DEFINING THE CUSTOMER'S MARKET

To be in a consultative relationship means that a salesman must be able to see the world as his customers see it. In the customer's world, *his* customers are kings. Because the 80–20 rule applies to a salesman's customers as well to his own company, it is more accurate to say that, in the customer's world, *his key-account customers* are kings. Every decision a salesman's customer makes about his business must, in the long run, be affected by the nature of his own key accounts and how well he knows and serves their needs. Only by learning as much as possible about these vital cornerstones of a customer's market can a salesman work with him on a close, continuing consultative basis to offer him profit improvement.

If he is to get inside his customer's market, the consultative salesman will have to equip himself with two fundamental market

definition skills. One is the ability to make a market-oriented needs
analysis of his customer's key accounts so that he knows the main
targets that his customer must market to. The second skill the
salesman requires is the knack of segmenting his customer's market into groups of the heaviest actual and potential users.

Market-oriented needs analysis. The consultative salesman
defines a customer's markets principally on the basis of their needs
for the benefit values of his customer's product and service systems. This does not mean that he ignores other classifications by
which markets may be defined, such as Standard Industrial Classifications (SIC) or combined demographic-psychographic classifications. But it does mean that he tries to see products and services
the way markets do: as solutions to needs. Therefore, these needs
must be made known, understood, and answered by the long-term
planning process that he practices with his key accounts.

Figure 3.1 shows four basic market need classifications
that many consultative salesmen have found helpful to work with.

THE ECONOMIES	THE PRESTIGES
1. Need to economize on money (thrift) 2. Need to economize on time and effort (convenience)	1. Need to be awarded a sense of inclusive-ness and being "in" 2. Need to be awarded a sense of exclusive-ness and being "one up"
THE IDENTITIES	THE VANITIES
1. Need to identify with modernity and venturesomeness 2. Need to identify with reliability, tradition, and conservatism	1. Need to display tangible vanities evidenced by physical possessions 2. Need to display intangible vanities evidenced by intellectual capabilities or achieve-ment

Figure 3.1   Four basic market need classifications.

They are not the only classes of needs, nor are they the only terms by which these particular needs can be defined. But they provide a good illustration of what the consultative salesman is in for when he sets about to make a needs analysis of a customer's market.

Market segmentation. In Figure 3.2, a 1-2-3-4 method is illustrated by which the consultative salesman can put his needs analysis to work. The figure covers the problem of identifying the highest potential market segment for a customer who manufactures and markets hydraulic power drives.

Step 1. The consultative salesman and his customer work together to segment out all original equipment manufacturers of construction machinery who need all types of power drives from all construction equipment manufacturers.

Step 2. The construction equipment manufacturers who need power drives are segmented according to the kind of product-oriented benefits they require. In this case, one segment needs the benefits of electrical power drives, another needs the benefits of mechanical drives, and a third needs—or may be persuaded to need—the benefits of hydraulic drives.

Step 3. The manufacturers who need the benefits of hydraulic power drives are further segmented according to the specific nature of the operating benefit they require. One segment primarily needs the money benefits of economy, which can be called thrift. Another segment needs the time and effort, or convenience, benefits of economy. A third segment needs the benefits of identifying with the modernity and venturesomeness associated with a progressive image.

Step 4. The actual and potential heavy users in each of these segments are further segmented. These are represented in Figure 3.2 as segments ME (money benefits of economy), CE (convenience benefits of economy), and IM (identification with the benefits of a modern image). It is these heavy users who will form the market base for the consultative salesman's long-term business planning relationship with his key account.

The exact same 1-2-3-4 method of market segmentation can be applied by the consultative salesman to his customer's customers. In "customer's customer country" in the figure, the seg-

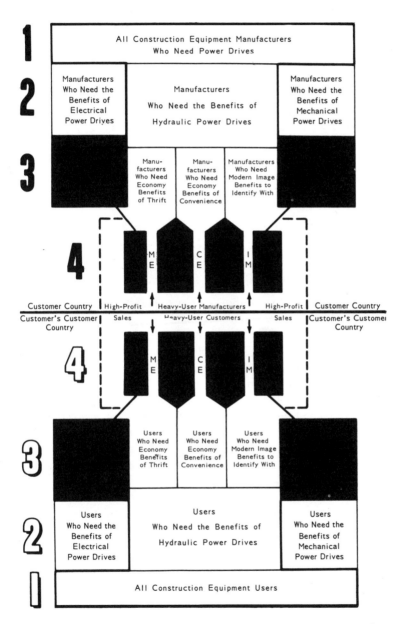

Figure 3.2   The consultative salesman's method of market segmentation.

mentation process moves from the bottom up beginning with all construction equipment users. It then narrows to the original equipment manufacturers' users who need the benefits of hydraulic power drives, then narrows further to users who need each of the specific benefits of hydraulic drives, and finally arrives at the heavy-user segments within each benefit category. It is these heavy-user customers who will form the account base for the consultative salesman's key customers. The interface that these heavy-user customers make with the heavy-using manufacturers is shown by the area in the figure that is enclosed in dotted lines. This is the ultimate source of the consultative salesman's heavy-profit business.

DEFINING THE CUSTOMER'S BUSINESS

Once the consultative salesman has defined a customer's market in terms of its major needs and the characteristics that segment out the heaviest needers from all others, he is ready to define the nature of his customer's business as a response to these needs. This is his basic business definition skill. He is required to practice it for three major reasons. First, remarkably few of his customers will know how to define their own businesses in a market-oriented manner. Second, unless both the salesman and his customer know what kind of business they are in from their end-user market's point of view, the customer's business cannot be planned for. There is a third reason, too. Unless the salesman's own company operates from an end-user's-eye view of its key-account businesses, it will not be able to supply either the information resource or the product and service systems which the consultative salesman requires for his operations.

There are two ways of looking at a customer's business from a market-oriented perspective. One is to define the customer as a moneymaker in a manner that shows the relationship of his income to his operations as a servicer of market needs. The other is to define the customer as a marketer. This will help reveal the basis of market acceptance that underpins the customer's business.

THE CUSTOMER AS A MONEYMAKER

If a salesman is going to be able to position himself as a consultant to the business of a key account, he must first learn the basic economics of the house the customer lives in. In order to improve a customer's profit, he has to know the size and nature of the profit he will be improving.

Figure 3.3 represents a typical customer's house of busi-

Figure 3.3 The house a customer lives in.

ness. A salesman who comes to call enters through the front door, shows his card, and is admitted to the competitive bidding action that takes place on the main floor. This is where the customer's currently marketed products or services are showcased. Somewhere among them are the 20 percent that supply the 80 percent of the customer's profitable sales volume. Identifying these relatively few big winners and planning to serve their requirements are a consultative salesman's first major tasks.

Upstairs, on the second floor of the customer's house, is his new products department. Above it is his research and development. Some of the new products that originate here may be marketed in the near-term future. In a growing business, new product income should be as much as 30 percent of total income at any given time. Yet the failure rate of new products is extraordinarily high. Whether as many as nine out of every ten new products fail, or only six out of ten, new product development is a failure-dominated function. The consultative salesman must get upstairs to the new products department on a regular basis so that he will be able to spot the comers, gear up his own company's development engineering, manufacturing, and marketing functions to serve their requirements, and contribute importantly to insuring their success so that he can have a major share in it.

So far, the consultative salesman has merely paralleled the call pattern of a sophisticated product salesman. He has called on the purchasing agents, buying committees, and perhaps product managers and market managers at their main floor location. He has gone upstairs to the new product department. He will also look in occasionally on the development activities still further up the stairs. But, as the figure indicates, this adds up to only one-half a regular call pattern for a consultative salesman. For him, no visualization of a customer's house is complete without an inspection of the cash flow machine that sits in the basement. Into it flows the income from sales of the customer's best-selling current products and the few new products that have survived into commercialization. These new product dollars are vitally necessary. They compensate for the erosion in earning power of older products which are continually falling out of the big winner's circle and entering the 80 percent of all products which make only a marginal contribution to net income.

Cash flow is defined as after-tax earnings plus depreciation. It indicates a company's net worth and where it comes from. Few salesmen ever get into a customer's basement to inspect his cash flow machine. Either they lack the credentials to make the trip or they do not recognize its value. A consultative salesman, however, must intimately understand the nature of his customer's cash circulation and devote his work to improving it.

Yet even this added source of information is not enough. No customer's cash flow machine stands alone. It always rests on a foundation, and the best name for this foundation is market acceptance: the need base in the customer's market which supports the entire house his business lives in. Defining a customer's business from the point of view of his market base is the second step in applying the consultative salesman's business definition skills.

THE CUSTOMER AS A MARKETER

The consultative salesman's mission of business definition for a key account has one overriding objective: to define the business in such a way that what it sells is revealed distinctly and apart from what it manufactures. The same thing can be said in another way. What its end users get out of doing business with the account must be separately pulled out from what the account puts into the products and services that generate the business. Only by knowing what meets the demand of his customer's customers can the consultative salesman plan to help his customers improve their profit from supplying them.

This means that the salesman will have to find ways to describe his customer's business as a supplier of benefit values to its heavy-user customers and not as a supplier of the physical product or service systems that provide the benefits. Since most businessmen think readily in terms of physical products or services, and much less readily in the terms that their markets use to describe the benefit values of products and services, market-orienting the definition of an ongoing business is never an easy task.

The market-oriented business description. To define a customer's business meaningfully—that is, in a manner the salesman
can plan for—the consultative salesman must follow a method that
often takes a deliberately contentious stand with his client. He
must state, and be prepared to act on, a premise like this:

Every time I hear you define your business in terms of a material, a
process, a product or service—anything other than a *market need* for
a *benefit value*—I'm going to say just one thing: "From the market's
point of view, there is no such business." Then we will work together
to learn just what kind of business it really may be.

This is very often a tough and unrelenting process, especially for customers who may be managerial doers rather than con-
ceptualizers. It can be a long way from the beginning of a business
definition process to an end point that enables a consultative salesman to help market-orient his customer and his own sales to him.
Once, for example, Eastern Airlines defined the nature of its business as "a business of mills—not dollars, not pennies, but mills"
which represent one-tenth of a cent. It has taken many years for
Eastern to be able to see that "Travel wasn't just the going and
the coming. It was the entire idea of living, working, or playing
somewhere else for a period of time. . . . What it has come to—
for the airlines and agents—is the sale of experiences."

An idea of the demands which market orientation can
make on the ingenuity and persistence—as well as the market concentrations—of the consultative salesman can be seen from the
following dialog. It represents a summary of a teaching session
in business definition conducted with a group of consultative
salesmen by Mack Hanan.

All right, sir. What kind of business are you in?
I'm in the hardware business.
For the sake of this dialog, please remember the point
of view I'm going to take. Every time I hear a business defined
in terms of products or processes or distribution systems—anything other than a market need—I'm going to say just one thing:
"From the market's point of view, there is no such business."

Now, "the hardware business" is a distribution-oriented definition. From the market's point of view, there is no such business.

Well, this is a fine time to tell me there is no such business as the hardware business. I've only been in it for a quarter of a century. Now, all of a sudden, there is no such business. Be that as it may, I'll go along. Suppose I put it this way. I make and sell traverse rods—curtain rods, as they're more familiarly known. Since they're made of hard, cold-rolled metal, I refer to them as hard ware. Get it? Hard ware, and that's why their major outlet is through hardware departments and stores. So let's say I'm in the curtain rod business.

There is no such business as the curtain rod business.

So now I'm unemployed. First you took me out of the hardware business. Now you take me out of the curtain rod business. I have no business at all. In two sentences, you accomplished what none of my competitors could do in 25 years.

Let's look at it this way. How's business in the so-called curtain rod business?

Now that's a question I can answer. Not good, I'm sorry to say. Not good at all.

What's the main reason?

It's very simple, really. We are suffering from unfair competition.

How do you define "unfair competition"?

Anybody who makes an inferior product and sells it at a lower price.

And how do you define an "inferior product"?

All products other than ours. I'm serious. We are the best—and by the best, I mean this: Our curtain rods are the strongest, longest-lasting, most durable curtain rods you can buy. Once they're up, they're up for good. That's why we've become the standard of the industry.

Then what's the problem?

Quality is expensive. That's the problem. We have a premium product and it carries a premium price. The inferior products carry an inferior price. And that's where the heart of our market is going—to the price brands.

Why should the heart of your market prefer an inferior product, no matter what the price is? If they buy a price brand, how can they get the strength and durability you offer?

That's just it. They're willing to sacrifice strength and durability for what the inferior rods give them.

What's that? Inferiority?

No. Attractiveness. Slimness. Streamlining. That's what they tell us the inferior curtain rods have that we don't have. What they really mean is cheapness, skimpiness, less metal, and more gingerbread.

Perhaps not. Perhaps they really mean attractiveness. Are they attractive?

Well, many of them are rather graceful looking, yes. They're fluted and sculptured. I suppose you could call them attractive.

Doesn't this suggest that the market sees these curtain rods as superior, not inferior, to yours? Superior, that is, in a benefit value you lack: attractiveness.

But they're inferior in the basic characteristics we have established for quality curtain rods: strength and durability.

But they may be superior in the basic characteristics the market has established for quality curtain rods: attractiveness and style. What kind of business would you say it is whose needs are for attractiveness and style?

The inferior curtain rod business.

Think of it from the market's point of view.

What can I call it? The attractiveness business?

How about the home beauty business, the fashionable-living business, the interior decoration business—maybe even the home environment business?

Me—a horny-handed hardware man—in the interior decoration business!

Defining a business from its market's point of view is one thing. Putting the definition to work is something else again. What does it mean to define a curtain rod manufacturer's business as an interior decoration business? For one thing, it creates the context for the consultative salesman's entire business planning process. It forces an answer to the question, "What kind of products, services, and promotional appeals best fit this kind of business?" In this case, it directs attention to the interiors business as the basis for growth in curtain rod sales. It avoids the product-oriented trap of planning to sell more curtain rods, which forces the emphasis onto the physical product and its manufacturing processes. Instead, it invites attention to the market-oriented opportunity of planning to serve the needs of the interior decoration market with decorative and functional systems that feature curtain rods and that can be progressively expanded to a wide variety of companion products and services. In this way, a market-oriented business definition can inspire new product creativity.

A second advantage comes from being able to "position" the full range of suppliers that are both indirectly and directly competitive with the curtain rod manufacturer. They emerge as all the suppliers of interior decoration and internal environmental systems that compete in any major way for the end-user's discretionary home improvement dollar. Once they are known, their marketing strategies can be planned against. Thus the trap of planning small—that is, only to match the benefit values of direct competition—can be avoided.

Most important of all, defining a business from the market's point of view opens the way to positioning the customer's products and processes as opportunities for profit improvement.

POSITIONING THE CUSTOMER'S PRODUCTS AND PROCESSES FOR PROFIT IMPROVEMENT

In working out a market-oriented definition of each account's business, the consultative salesman has one objective in mind: to help his accounts maximize the profit they can achieve from the product and service systems they provide for their own key customers' needs. In the course of carrying out this task, the salesman will be motivated by two considerations: (1) to help his key customers plan to *minimize* their investment in the product and service systems that must yield their budgeted profit; (2) to help his own company plan to *maximize* the profit it receives from the sale of its product and service systems to his key accounts.

In this way the consultative salesman helps his customers to keep down their costs of engineering, manufacturing, and marketing. He also enables them to preempt their markets' business as much as possible through products and services tailored to their users' needs. Simultaneously, he helps his company keep its own profits up and its cost of sales down.

The consultative salesman has two ways of keeping down his customers' costs and, at the same time, custom-tailoring their selling systems to zero in on their heavy-user market needs. One way is by helping to make sure that their products are not overengineered and therefore overcosted. The other way is by making sure that the materials, processes, products, and services of his customers can deliver the major benefits that their customers prefer. His knowledge of market needs is his prime asset in this task. This knowledge will help him recommend the most marketable positioning for his customers' existing product and service lines. It will further guide him in counseling on the positioning of new products and services that they have projected in their business plans.

Since many of these products and services will contain ingredients and components purchased from the consultative salesman's company, his stake in his customers' new product success is every bit as great as theirs. Whenever one of their new products fails, he and his company are deprived of a potential profit opportunity. Everything he can do to improve the success ratio of new products from the typical one or two out of ten can add significantly to his company's profit. And if he can help his customers generate ideas for profitable new products that they would not have created without his aid, he can even further enhance the added value of his contribution.

POSITIONING FOR PROFIT IMPROVEMENT

As he negotiates his way into a long-term account relationship with his key customers, the consultative salesman will face a recurrent problem: How does he know where to keep looking to offer profit improvement? The answer to this question lies in his ability to position his account's products and services so that the opportunity for improved profit will become clearly apparent.

When a product or a process has been positioned, several things have happened to it. More important than anything else, it has been flushed out of hiding. It has been located, identified, and targeted. It has also been assigned some order of magnitude. It can be regarded as a potential big winner, an also-ran, or something in between. And it can be put in a priority rank order as to when the salesman will attack it.

Whether a key account is a product manufacturer or service supplier, the salesman will find that *life-cycling* his account's products and services can best highlight the opportunities they offer for profit improvement. Through life-cycling them, he can quickly see where each product stands in its contribution to income over time. He can see which products need help. And because new products are susceptible to profit improvement approaches different from those of growth products or mature products, the salesman will be able to tailor-make his miniplans to fit the exact requirements of each situation once he has cycled its location on a time-and-income curve.

In addition to exploring an account's products and services for profit improvement opportunities, the salesman will find it rewarding to penetrate deeply into the vital processes by which they come into being. In this way he will be able to seek out the needs of each process for greater cost effectiveness. Of all the processes, a customer's marketing process can be the most fertile source of opportunity. Any contribution the salesman can make to helping his customer upgrade market demand can lead directly to profit improvement.

Life-cycling analysis of product opportunities

The salesman's basic positioning tool in seeking profit improvement opportunities within a manufacturing account or service supplier is the product life cycle curve. It is the best device a salesman can have to bring out the principal product areas where profit improvement proposals will have the most favorable chance of being accepted by his customers.

An idealized life cycle curve is shown in Figure 3.4. It illustrates the sales power of a product on a year-by-year basis over five years of its life. After incurring its original research and development costs, which resulted in a net loss before taxes, the product has been able to pay the costs back since market entry by returning a profit in the form of the sales dollars it has earned above and beyond the breakeven point. In achieving its payback, the product has passed through three major phases of life: birth as a commercial entity, growth into a winner, and maturity.

Once past breakeven, the figure shows that the product moved into "brand country," where its demand pull enabled it to command premium price acceptance. It sold at list, or perhaps even above. Profits outran sales. On the downside of the curve, the product fell into "commodity country." Its once-unique bene-

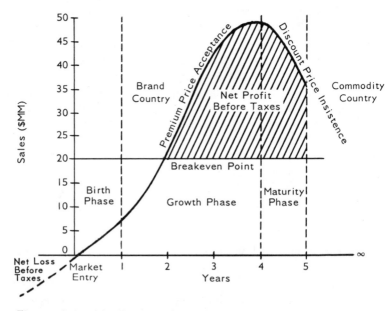

Figure 3.4 Idealized product life cycle.

fits were neutralized by competition or made obsolete by technological innovation. Since its initial benefits had been discounted, its market insisted that it also sell at a discount. List price became a memory and sales exceeded profits.

This idealized life curve is paralleled by most successful products. Unsuccessful products rarely make it much past breakeven. Instead of enjoying a growth phase, they die young. For the most part, the growth phase is the zone of major profit contribution. Therefore, it can be said that the consultative salesman's task as far as product positioning is concerned is threefold: (1) he must help his customer's new products survive their birth phase and achieve growth; (2) he must help growth products maximize their growth in terms of how high and how fast they climb, how long they remain on top, and how slowly they decline; and (3) he must help mature products slow down their decline or he must help turn them around toward new growth. These are the consultative salesman's three basic options. He has a fourth option as well. At any phase of its life cycle, he can help reduce a product's cost base and thereby lower its breakeven point. This, too, can improve its profit.

There are four steps for the salesman to take in life-cycling the profit improvement opportunities offered by his customer's key products: target his account's key products which are also vital to him, generate a supply of life cycle curves, position key products in their life cycles, and then create a master curve of his major opportunities.

Step 1. The salesman should make a list of his account's key products or services. Then he should add to it the potential winners that may become key products over the next 12 to 24 months. Together, these will be among the products and services which contribute to the 80 percent of the account's profitable sales volume according to the 80–20 rule. Then the salesman should subtract from the list any products or services for which he does not act as an important supplier. What he will be left with is a target list of products or services that are vital to his account as well as to himself. Any profit improvement he can add to them will be important to him and to his customer. He therefore knows in advance that his work will provide a sound base of reciprocal self-interest.

Step 2. The salesman should then draw up a supply of product life cycle curves like the one in Figure 3.4. The curve will fit almost every business except outright fads. Only the length of the intervals on the time axis may differ. The salesman will have to adjust the intervals to fit his customer's industry. In consumer goods, for example, a three- to five-year life cycle is common. In heavy industrial products, life cycles may double or triple this length.

Step 3. On each curve the salesman should position one of the products on his key list. To do so, he will need to know or be able to perceive three facts. The first one is the simplest; it is the length of time the product or service has been on the market. A two-year-old product, for instance, is positioned at ME—the point of market entry—plus two. The second fact is the

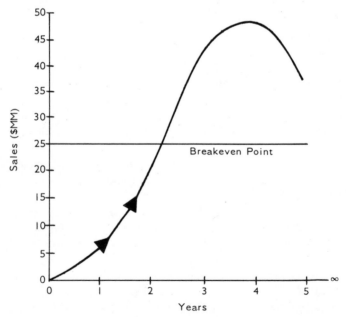

Figure 3.5   New product positionings on the life cycle curve.

product's approximate dollar sales volume. The third fact is its probable breakeven point. To obtain these figures, the salesman will have to rely on the cooperation of his account or on approximations he will be able to perceive for himself about industry and competitive performance norms.

Step 4. The salesman will come out of step 3 with a collection of product positionings which resemble Figures 3.5, 3.6, and 3.7. Figure 3.5 shows the position of two new products which have not yet broken even. Figure 3.6 shows two growth products. Figure 3.7 shows two mature products that may or may not be nearing the end of their life cycles. The salesman should superimpose these three curves one on top of the other so that he can draw one master curve. This will give him a composite picture of his account's key product mix as it relates in a given moment of time

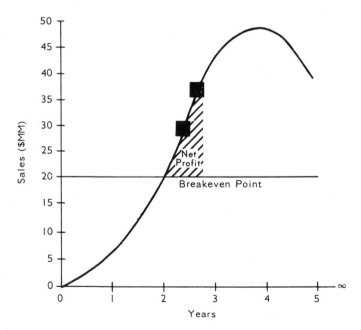

Figure 3.6 Growth product positionings on the life cycle curve.

to what he himself is selling. A master curve is shown in Figure 3.8. Since the marketplace is dynamic, the salesman should re-create a master curve at least annually so that he can track each product's movement over the curve as if it were a moving picture, which it really is, rather than a still picture.

INTERPRETING A CUSTOMER'S PRODUCT POSITIONING

The master life cycle curve in Figure 3.8 is the consultative salesman's most important blueprint for the profit improvement planning he will put into operation with a key account. If there is one piece of paper that can influence the contribution of his performance more than all others, this is it. But creating it is only the beginning. The salesman must learn how to interpret it too.

Looking at the master life cycle curve as a bird's-eye view

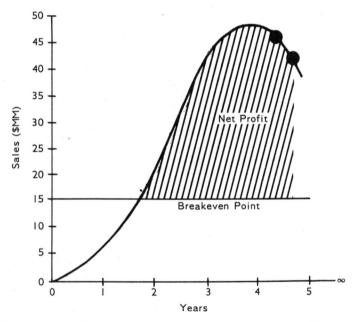

Figure 3.7   Mature product positionings on the life cycle curve.

of the salesman's opportunity with his account, a broad range of interpretations can be made of the gross dimensions of his opportunity. They will all focus on one or both of two objectives: to help prolong profitable product life cycles that already exist and to help initiate profitable new life cycles. The precise strategies for capitalizing on these objectives will find their expression in the consultative salesman's profit improvement miniplans.

Interpreting an account's overall opportunity from the master curve. From the consultative salesman's point of view, the account whose master curve is illustrated in Figure 3.8 appears as a business with two new products in group A that are still below their breakeven point, two apparent growth products in group B that may continue on to become "shooting stars," and two apparently mature products in group C that are generating the bulk

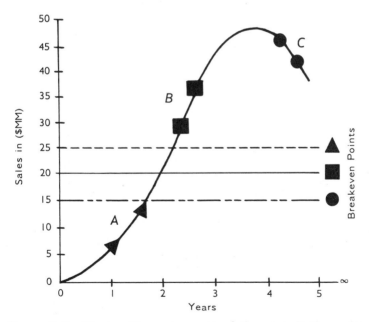

Figure 3.8   Master life cycle curve of the consultative salesman's opportunities.

of the account's cash flow. This overview gives the salesman a great variety of options to work with.

Interpreting an account's new product opportunities from the master curve. New products carry the highest degree of risk. The two shown in group A have not yet paid out. They may not. New products are always heavily laden, carrying the burden of their net loss before taxes which was incurred by their development up to the point of market entry. These costs are then further burdened by generally high introductory marketing expenses. The odds against new product success suggest that it is unlikely for both of the group A entries to break even. Anything the salesman can do to decrease their risk of failure will be extremely important to his account.

As a rule, there are three strategies he can consider to improve their chance of reaching a breakeven point and returning a profit: (1) increase the speed with which the new products move up the sales curve; (2) increase the steepness of their angle of climb; (3) decrease their breakeven point by reducing some of their cost burden. Since new products are cost-heavy, any strategies that add further costs will probably encounter customer resistance. This is why the salesman will find that the option of cost reduction will generally be best received by an account.

Interpreting an account's growth product opportunities from the master curve. Growth products appear the easiest to work with, but in practice they can be the hardest for the salesman to get at. Because growth products are so fraught with potential, few accounts are willing to rock the boat in any way as long as their shooting stars continue on course. The salesman's promise of profit improvement for group B must be more than worth the risk which may be perceived in any of the five strategies he can consider: (1) Increase the speed with which the growth products grow. (2) Increase the steepness of the angle of their climb. (3) Prolong the length of time they remain at the peak of their climb. (4) Help them plateau off their peak more slowly. (5) Decrease their breakeven point by reducing some of their cost burden.

In Figure 3.9 the profit improvement effect of four of these strategies is illustrated. The added profit at point *a* comes from increasing the steepness of the growth curve. Point *b* shows added profit from prolonging the curve's peak. At *c,* a plateau slows the product's drop-off from its peak so profit can continue. And at *d,* new profit results from a lowered breakeven point.

Interpreting an account's mature product opportunities from the master curve. The mature products in group C represent the only certainty on the master curve and usually offer excellent opportunities for the consultative salesman. Because they are successful products they give the salesman something to work with that is his greatest asset: a strong knowledge base about their market needs and preferences. He also has money to work with on his account's side since these products have demonstrated market acceptance, and, as their reward, they have become the major contributors to the account's cash flow. They possess another

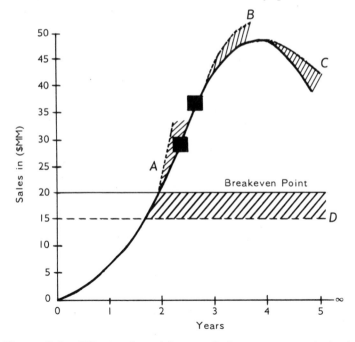

Figure 3.9   Effects of applying profit improvement strategies.

unique attribute. Most of their original cost burden has probably long ago been amortized. Their current operating cost should also be relatively low. It will probably be more difficult, therefore, for the salesman to find ways of appreciably lowering the cost of group C products than to propose profit improvement strategies that may add to their cost. He nonetheless has four major strategies to consider: (1) Decrease the speed with which the mature products decline down their sales curve. (2) Decrease the steepness of the angle of their decline. (3) Renovate them enough to turn them around into second-generation shooting stars entering a new growth phase. (4) Decrease their breakeven points by reducing some of their cost burden.

Altogether, these interpretations of the salesman's opportunity to plan profit improvement for his account yield a dozen options for him to explore. From them, he can work up his custom-tailored miniplans to present his strategies for seizing the options he selects.

As he constructs the life cycle curves of his customer's products or services, the consultative salesman has an excellent opportunity to ask questions. How long has this new product been in its present position on the curve? Did it climb quickly or slowly? Faster or slower than the norm? Or has it been moving upward haltingly? What about the well-established products in the C category: what is their track record over the past five years? Have the shooting stars in the B category leveled off? Or are they still shooting upward? Questions like these are designed to place the life cycle curve's snapshot view of today within a time frame where the dynamics of the customer's business can be revealed.

Cost-effectiveness analysis of process opportunities

Processes can have life cycles too. When they do, they are also susceptible to life cycle analysis. Many processes, however, are far more enduring than products. Not only may they last longer in their most productive state, sometimes for a decade or more, but they are usually far more heavily weighted with fixed costs. This fact makes them especially worthwhile targets for cost reduction.

In Figure 3.10 a four-stage profit improvement approach is shown for equipment designed to affect the cleaning and finishing processes by which parts made of metal, plastic, rubber, and other materials are readied for assembly and installation.

At stage 1 the total incremental investment which would be required by the purchase and installation of the salesman's equipment is itemized. Stage 2 sets down the annual contribution to profit improvement which the equipment can make, in terms of either a net decrease in operating cost or a net increase in revenue. Stage 3 has two parts. In *A* is calculated the effect of the salesman's equipment on operating costs. In *B* the salesman can demonstrate the effect of his equipment on revenues. Finally, in stage 4 the equipment's profit return is figured on the incremental investment required to obtain it. In the figure a before-tax rate of return of roughly 86 percent is arrived at on the basis of a $24,952 projected profit improvement. This earmarks an exceptionally good opportunity for the salesman to pursue.

Life-cycling analysis and cost-effectiveness analysis enable

Figure 3.10 A four-stage profit improvement approach.

STAGE 1. INCREMENTAL INVESTMENT ANALYSIS

1. Cost of proposed equipment	$39,600		
Estimated installation cost	6,000		
Subtotal	$45,600		
Minus initial tax benefit of	3,190		
Total		$42,410	1
2. Disposal value of equipment to be replaced	8,000		
Capital additions required in absence of proposed equipment	6,000		
Minus initial tax benefit for capital additions of	420		
Total		$13,580	2
3. Incremental investment (1 − 2)		$28,830	3

Figure 3.10   (continued)

STAGE 2. PROFIT IMPROVEMENT ANALYSIS
(ANNUAL CONTRIBUTION)

4. Profit improvement — net decrease in operating costs (from line 27)	$24,952	4
5. Profit improvement — net increase in revenue (from line 31)	$	5
6. Annual profit improvement (lines 4 + 5)	$24,952	6

STAGE 3. NEXT YEAR OPERATING BENEFITS
FROM PROPOSED EQUIPMENT

A. Effect of proposed equipment on operating costs

(*Computed on Machine-Hour Basis*)	*Present*	*Proposed*	
7. Direct labor (wages plus incentives and bonuses)	$ 10.50	$ 3.50	7
8. Indirect labor (supervision, inspectors, helpers)	3.67	1.22	8
9. Fringe benefits (vacations, pensions, insurance, etc.)	2.15	0.72	9
10. Maintenance (ordinary only, parts and labor)	1.18	0.90	10
11. Abrasives, media, compounds, or other consumable supplies	1.32	1.10	11
12. Power	0.56	0.48	12
13. Total (sum of 7 through 12)	$ 19.38	$ 7.92	13
14. Estimated machine hours to be operated next year	2,400	3,000	14
15. Partial operating costs next year (13 × 14)	$46,512 (A)	$23,760 (B)	15
16. Partial operating profit improvement (15A — 15B)		$22,752	16

Figure 3.10   (continued)

(*Computed on a Yearly Basis*)	Increase	Decrease	
17. Scrap or damaged work	$	$ 700	17
18. Down time		1,500	18
19. Floor space			19
20. Subcontracting			20
21. Inventory			21
22. Safety			22
23. Flexibility			23
24. Other			24
25. Total	$ (A)	$ 2,200 (B)	25
26. Net decrease in operating costs (partial) (25B — 25A)		$ 2,200	26
27. Total effect of proposed equipment on operating costs (16 + 26)		$24,952	27

B. Effect of proposed equipment on revenue

(*Computed on Yearly Basis*)	Increase	Decrease	
28. From change in quality of products	$	$	28
29. From change in volume of output			29
30. Total	$ (A)	$ (B)	30
31. Net increase in revenue (30A — 30B)		$	31

STAGE 4. ANALYSIS OF RETURN ON INCREMENTAL INVESTMENT

32. Incremental investment (line 3)	$28,830	32
33. Annual profit improvement (line 6)	$24,952	33
34. Before-tax return on investment (line 33 ÷ line 32)	86%	34

the consultative salesman to create the data base from which he can put together his miniplan presentations to his accounts. As a result of these types of analyses, he can anticipate an alert and interested hearing by his accounts since he is addressing himself to proven areas of their needs.

BANKING THE CUSTOMER INFORMATION RESOURCE

Information is the consultative salesmen's prime resource. Without it, or without the ability to manage its application, no salesman can operate in a consultative manner.

The salesman's task is to amass information about his customer's market, business, products, and processes, together with the external factors that affect them, and incorporate these data into every aspect of his account service. His payoff, however, comes only when he capitalizes his information in the form of adding the value of profit improvement to his customer's operations. Used in this way, information takes on a catalytic role for the salesman who sells consultatively.

The term *data bank,* which is often used to refer to the salesman's knowledge resource, is an appropriate one. A data bank is much like a money bank. It requires continual deposits to keep it solvent. Withdrawals from it quite literally finance consultative selling, since they provide the salesman with four vital advantages.

1. Information is the salesman's ticket of admission to each consultative relationship. It gets him in the door by allowing him to represent himself as possessing the added value of knowing something that can be helpful.

2. Information is the salesman's medium of exchange in return for information he needs from his account. The only way the salesman can get important customer information is by giving important information to his customer. By earning the right to this information, the salesman earns the right to consult.

3. Information is the basis for the profit improvement objectives the salesman will set with his customers since it is the source of the assumptions he must make that underlie his objectives.

4. Information is the foundation of the multiresource service capabilities with which the salesman and his company must surround a consultative account. It is also his entry wedge into the multifunction customer access he must have within each key business to which he sells.

THE TICKET OF ADMISSION

When a consultative salesman makes his first appearance on the threshold of a key account, he is naked except for the knowledge box that he holds under his arm and his pretension that he can use it to add unique values. Information allows the salesman to have an answer to the first screening question he must anticipate: "What do *you* know that I don't know?" If the salesman's response is knowledgeable—that is, if he is able to demonstrate a knowledge of the customer's business problems and their solutions—the salesman may get in the door. Information is his only ticket. Since everything he does thereafter will be based on it, he must present it first before he can speak credibly about profit improvement.

The salesman's information allows a customer to suspend his disbelief that the salesman can help him consultatively. As Figure 3.11 shows, it enables the salesman to begin the vital confidence-continuity cycle on which the longevity of his entire customer relationship will depend. Once into the cycle, his information resource helps him stay in by giving him a means to answer the next expected question: "What you have to say is interesting. Now, what can you do about it for *me?*" The profit improvement project that the salesman can suggest in response marks his first step on the road to building the climate of confidence that permits continuity.

THE MEDIUM OF EXCHANGE

In a consultative selling relationship, a familiar ground rule applies: The salesman gets nothing for nothing. To the extent that he requires information from his key customers to help him in his profit planning, he must provide a quid pro quo which will open the customer's knowledge bank to him. To get at this information resource, he must first introduce his own.

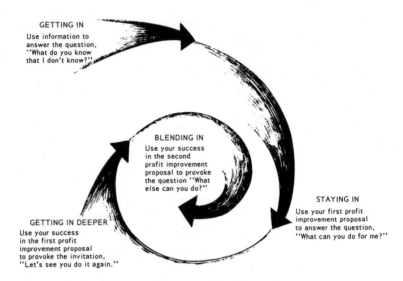

Figure 3.11 The confidence-continuity cycle.

The information he gets back from his customers will generally be in direct proportion to what he brings to them. If he offers information that is relevant and current and that adds a perceived value to what the customer already knows, he is likely to receive information that is meaningful and timely to him and adds value to his planning. Depth is usually met by depth and shallowness by shallowness.

If the salesman's information is irrelevant or obsolete there can be no trade-off. Not only will he not receive customer information in return. He will probably have directed at him the two most dreaded questions a consultative salesman can face: Who? and Why? "Who," his customer will ask him, "*are* you, anyway?" and "Why are you calling on *me?*"

THE SOURCE OF ASSUMPTIONS

A profit improvement plan's objectives are its warhead. The rest of the plan exists to serve it. The plan's strategies are the action elements that make it go and the plan's controls make sure that the strategies are operating and the plan is on course. Since objectives are based on assumptions, and since assumptions come out of the salesman's information resource, information is actually the ultimate source of a plan's energy.

To say that a plan is as good as its objectives is therefore to say that it is as good as the information base that permits the underlying assumptions to be made.

A good information base will not rule out the unknowable factors that will influence the evolution of a plan's strategies. Nor will it make them knowable. By definition, a plan's unknowables become known only ex post facto. The contribution of good information, however, is to reduce the risk that the plan's major assumptions will be badly off their mark. Inaccurate assumptions are the overwhelming reason why plans fail. Every added degree of accuracy in the assumptive process therefore gives a plan an added chance for success.

THE FOUNDATION OF SERVICE

In order to function consultatively, a salesman must call widely and deeply on the main decision makers and influencers in his key-account organizations. At each level he must be able to present himself as a literate businessman; that is, he must have something meaningful to say. He will also be required to have something meaningful to do. What he says and does will come directly from his information base.

A second aspect of the consultative salesman's role is to open up his own company's multiresource service capabilities to his key accounts. He will have to be knowledgeable about which services to call in to help solve each customer problem he takes on. He will also need to know enough about each service to monitor it acceptably and to manage its harmonious integration into his total system of services. The salesman's information base is therefore not only the foundation of his own service to customers. It is also his basis for managing the application of all other services he brings to bear on an account.

THE KNOWABLES

An account knows two types of information about itself better than anyone else does. One is about its own products and services. The other is about the key processes that generate them.

These are the two major areas of information that almost any account can say it really knows. All else it must estimate, suspect, theorize about. It stands to reason, then, that the consultative salesman should treat each of his accounts as the horse's mouth on these subjects.

The salesman's product knowledge will come mainly through life cycle analysis. The three processes he will have to get into are his account's marketing, manufacturing, and finance.

To bring profit improvement opportunities to an account's *marketing process,* a consultative salesman will have to know enough about it to contribute to its cost reduction and add to its sales income. His principal strategies will include providing information on economic trends and market needs that can be translated into new sales leads as well as counseling on techniques for improving quality control of sales, distribution, advertising, and other customer marketing operations. He may also suggest market research studies to update or validate end-user knowledge that can be executed by the customer alone or jointly with his own company on a cooperative basis. A further strategy is to supply innovative products or services that can give the customer a branded competitive edge in his marketing.

To bring profit improvement opportunities to a key account's *manufacturing process,* a consultative salesman will have to know enough about it to contribute to its cost reduction through such strategies as process redesign, introduction of new or substitute materials, installation of new operating efficiencies, reduction of yield losses or byproduct reclamation, application of his knowledge of market needs to help eliminate or avoid product overengineering, or even offering the more cost-effective alternative of buying some product components instead of producing them through self-manufacture.

The testimony of one salesman for an environmental systems manufacturer dramatically illustrates the advantages of knowing an account's manufacturing process.

What I need the most is more extensive knowledge of specific facets of my customers' processes that must be subjected to air pollution control. As an example, all cement kilns require air pollution control equipment. There are, however, wet kilns, dry kilns, and several other variations such as conventionally fired or air preheated kilns. Basic knowledge of these processes would enable me to establish rapport, or at least a degree of comfort, with a prospective customer. I could "talk his language" well enough to make a solid equipment recommendation and back this up with facts as to why I picked equipment type A rather than equipment type B.

To bring profit improvement opportunities to an account's *financial process,* a consultative salesman will have to know enough about it to help effect savings. He can help set up predictable patterns of volume purchasing and delivery. Or he can contribute to improved methods of customer inventory control or even handle some or all inventory control functions for his customers.

There are, of course, two other customer processes on which a consultative salesman can bring profit improvement approaches to bear. New product development and R&D can often be affected favorably by applications of the salesman's market knowledge at critical stages in the creative work. For the most part, however, the consultative salesman will find that his greatest leverage in fulfilling his promise of profit improvement comes from applying himself to his customer's marketing process. This is the area where he can have the most significant effect on improving customer income as opposed to solely introducing cost reductions. Since no company can consistently save its way to solvency, customer growth—and, along with it, the consultative salesman's own earnings growth—must ultimately come from opening up new sources of profitable sales. This must be the objective of the vast majority of the salesman's miniplans.

THE UNKNOWABLES

Every business faces far more unknowables than knowables. This fact alone can make any business a game. The consultative salesman is not expected to be able to know a customer's unknowables when the customer himself cannot. But the salesman must be aware of what the unknowables are and their likelihood of threatening the achievement of his profit improvement plans.

No matter what businesses they are in, all accounts must live with a similar set of five unknowables. They can be summarized as follows.

1. *Market needs*. Will significant changes occur in the market needs that form the base of our business demand? If so, will they occur quickly or slowly, openly or covertly, in the direction of our capabilities and the market values they provide or away from them?

2. *Competition*. Will the offerings of current competitors be improved so that they equal or exceed the perceived market value of our own? Will new competitors with new technologies or new marketing strategies enter our markets, destroying their balance or introducing novel market values?

3. *The economy*. When the business cycle moves, which way will it go? How far will it go, and how fast? Will it plateau? If so, for how long?

4. *Legislation*. Will federal, state, or local codes affecting our products or services impose cost-ineffective compliance on our operations to the detriment of our cost-price-value relationships or even the continued survival of the business?

5. *Technology*. Will technological breakthroughs in the form of new materials or new processes make the market value of our offerings obsolete or even preempt our very business base itself?

By sharing information with his accounts about the unknowables, the salesman can always make a contribution to them. No account can ever have enough hard facts in this area of its business. Nor can the unknowables ever become known in advance. Just as they seem to become apparent, they change. Yet some way must be found to collect the facts, store them, and feed them into the salesman's planning process.

THE CUSTOMER INFORMATION CENTER

A customer information center is a tool for banking the knowables along with sophisticated assumptions about the unknowables so that they can be used by the consultative salesman. Figure 3.12 shows a center based on six resource capabilities relat-

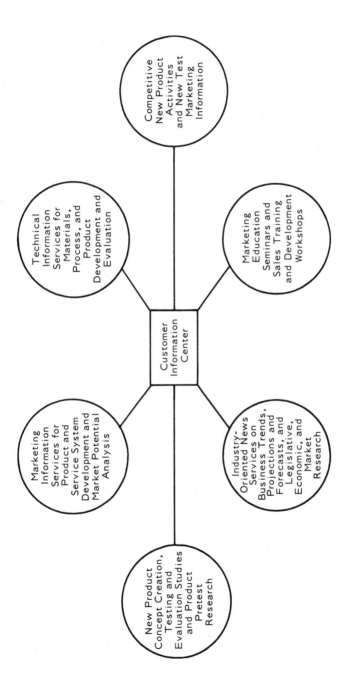

Figure 3.12 Customer information center.

ing to the business of a salesman's company and its key customers. These capabilities include marketing information, consultation, and research services; technical information, consultation, and research services; industry-oriented legislative, economic, and market research; competitive intelligence; and a wide variety of other news and education services. Services such as these give the consultative salesman important added values to sell. Their availability also adds to the value of the salesman himself, making his services more authoritative and more applicable by his customers. For his company, of course, the information center's existence creates a further opportunity for new income when it is managed as a profit center.

MAKING THE MINIPLAN

Because the consultative salesman is a line operating manager, he must adhere to the managerial maxim to plan his work with each key account and then work his plan. This means that he will have to squeeze out all the fat from the planning process, miniaturize it in the interests of his own limited preparatory time and his need to operate from it on a day-to-day basis, and come up with a business tool that will serve as many purposes as possible in a single document. A yearly miniplan offers him these benefits. It strips a business plan to its essentials. It rarely exceeds ten pages. Its basic information and format can be used by the salesman to serve as (1) his guidebook for managing his company's business with an account for each 12-month period, (2) his presentation to the account, and (3) his request for authorization and funds from his own management.

In Figure 3.13 an annual profit improvement miniplan is outlined. It begins with the single most important part of the plan, its *objectives*. These are the salesman's promises to add profit to his key account. Underlying his objectives are the assumptions he makes about the unknowables he cannot control but whose probable effects he nonetheless must make educated guesses about.

The second major component of a miniplan is the *strategy mix* which provides the procedures for the salesman to use in fulfilling the promise of his objectives. The consultative salesman's strategies will be composed of his profit improvement projects. Each project will have to outline the customer applications the salesman proposes to bring to bear on his account. To support them, he will also have to document the internal implementations to be made inside his own company.

The third part of the miniplan is the *controls and con-*

Figure 3.13   Profit improvement miniplan.

I. OBJECTIVES
(promises to add profit)

Profit Improvement Objectives
1. Added net profit: Expressed as added dollars and added percentage of profit contributed to earnings
2. Added return on investment: Expressed as added percentage contribution to ROI

Contributory Objectives
1. If the marketing process is to be affected by adding sales revenue: Expressed as added dollar volume, added unit volume, and added percent of market share contributions
2. If the marketing, manufacturing, or financial processes are to be affected by subtracting operating costs: Expressed as dollar contribution and percentage contribution to reduced costs

II. STRATEGIES
(profit improvement projects to fulfill promises)

1. Customer applications
2. Internal implementations
3. Time and budget frames

III. CONTROLS AND CONTINGENCIES
(proof that promises can be fulfilled)

1. Monitoring system
2. Measurement schedule
3. Contingencies

---

tingencies the salesman will have to set up to monitor and measure the progress of his plan, to offer proof that its promises are being fulfilled, and to have remedies on hand if they are not.

A ten-page maximum length can be adhered to if miniplans are constructed on this outline in the following way:

Objectives	1 page
Assumptions	1 page
Customer application strategies	3 pages
Internal implementation strategies	2 pages
Time and budget frames	1 page
Controls and contingencies	2 pages

OBJECTIVES

Customer question they answer:
Where are you taking my business?
Assurance they give:
To an added profit of $x or $x\%$.

There are two sets of objectives which are important for the consultative salesman to set down in his miniplan. The primary set is his *profit improvement objectives.* These can be expressed in terms of the added dollars or added percentage of new profit that he can contribute to his customers. The added percentage return on investment brought about by these new profits should also be targeted. One of the most important contributions to this investment base will be the costs of the miniplan's profit improvement strategies and their controls.

It is valuable for the salesman to set his profit improvement objectives on a best case/worst case basis. The best case is the maximum amount of profit improvement that his miniplan can generate if all the plan's assumptions prove correct, if every one of its strategies works as planned, and if no constraints inhibit their operation. The worst case, on the other hand, shows the minimal profit improvement that can be promised if the plan's performance is only average. The worst case must always be acceptable before a plan can safely be put to work.

The secondary set of objectives is the salesman's *contribu-*

tory objectives. These are the added sales revenues or reduced operating costs which will yield the planned profit improvement. If the consultative salesman chooses to affect a customer's marketing process by adding to its revenues, his contributory objectives will be sales objectives. They will be expressed as added dollar volume, added unit volume, and added percent of market share contributions. If the salesman decides to affect his customer's costs instead of revenues, he can work on the customer's marketing, manufacturing, or financial processes. His contributory objectives will then be expressed as the dollar and percentage contributions he can make by reducing expenditures.

By examining the numbers which he enters in his contributory and profit improvement objectives, the salesman can make a generally accurate estimate about the life cycle stage of the product or service he is planning for. Older products are better contributors of sales volume than profits. Newer products usually contribute more profits than sales. They are also more susceptible to cost cutting strategies than older products whose costs have been squeezed out of them. The consultative salesman should remember these rules of thumb in planning his objectives so that they can be kept in close relationship with reality.

Criteria. The consultative salesman must be certain that his miniplan's objectives can stand the test when he regularly measures them against five major criteria.

First of all, the plan's objectives must be achievable in the short run. This may seem so obvious as to be ignored. Yet more plans fail because their objectives are unachievable within a reasonably early time frame than for any other reason except faulty assumptions.

Second, objectives must be significant. Even if the best-case objectives are achievable, they may not be worth achieving. The best case may not be good enough, especially when it is compared against other potential objectives that could be targeted by other plans.

Third, the worst-case objectives must be acceptable. Even if the plan achieves only its minimal objectives, they must still make the best contribution that can possibly be made. If the worst-case objectives are unacceptable, the plan is also unacceptable.

Fourth, objectives must be commensurate with risk. A significant objective deserves an equal risk. But the risk should not normally so far exceed the probable reward that the plan becomes a game of chance. Barring unique circumstances, high-risk objectives should be shunned even though they promise high rewards. A low-reward objective at high risk is folly.

Fifth, objectives must be not only beneficial in the short run but free from causing long-term detriment. A profit objective achieved today at the cost of damaging an account's long-term image in a key market may very well be the most unprofitable commitment a salesman and his customer can make.

Ruling out debate. Consultative selling affords a salesman the option of selling his profit improvement objectives instead of his strategies. Traditional product selling, on the other hand, forces salesmen to sell the alleged superiorities of their strategies—optimistically alluded to as benefits—on a highly competitive basis. Instead of ruling out debate on the merits, selling the benefits of individual strategies invites heated and protected debate as to which competitor offers better benefits. Eventually all competitors offer similar benefits in an attempt to avoid losing the debate. Once a salesman's benefits are paralleled by competition, he will probably be forced to rely on price as his main sales incentive. This is the way that benefit selling leads inevitably to price selling.

A consultative salesman can sell his plan's objectives because he is able to position himself as a problem solver. As such, his objectives are designed to help solve his account's need for improved profit. If he performs his function properly, he can achieve the ultimate goal of his presentation: He can gain acceptance for the objectives of his plan and thereby rule out debate on the merits of their strategies.

Assumptions. To support the contention that his plan's objectives are achievable in the short run, the salesman must document them with the principal assumptions he is making about the elements of risk he can never calculate with certainty. His assumptions can help answer an important question relative to his objectives: "What makes you think so?" The answer his assumptions give should suggest as strongly as possible: "I know your business."

If a consultative salesman is going to promise profit improvement to a key account, he must be prepared to tape out the assumptions which underlie his promise and assign a percentage level of confidence to each of them. Some of the assumptions he will make will be on the positive side. If they prove true, they will aid the plan's achievement of its objectives. On the other end of the equation are negative assumptions. If they become realities, achievement of the plan's objectives will be impeded or perhaps even entirely prevented. The plan's success therefore becomes contingent on their not happening. There is a third class of assumptions which can be the most destructive. These are the sleepers, the potentially negative assumptions that the salesman forgets to include in his plan or that are not even triggered by his information base. When sleepers come out of nowhere and defeat a plan, the salesman pays the highest possible price for the information they teach him.

In defense of his objectives, the consultative salesman will have to make something like the following assumptive comments in his plan.

The profit improvement objectives in this plan are based on seven assumptions.

1. There is a 90 percent probability that the product and service system to be marketed according to this plan is in phase A of early growth in its life cycle and that it will not enter phase B of maturity during the plan's time frame.

2. There is a 60 percent probability that the time frame required by this plan will afford sufficient lead time to isolate its product and service system from competitive retaliation before profit improvement objectives have been achieved.

3. There is a 60 percent probability that market needs for the product and service system contained in this plan will intensify and a 90 percent probability that they will do no worse than remain at their present level of insistence on fulfillment.

4. There is an 80 percent probability that the business

cycle will continue on its high-level plateau for the entire duration of the plan's time frame. If any significant change were to occur, there is an 80 percent probability that it will be slightly upward.

5. There is a 10 percent probability that one new competitor will enter our market during the plan's time frame. Because of the nature of his capabilities and market image, he is most likely to adversely affect the market shares of competitors *A* and *B* rather than our own.

6. There is a 90 percent probability that no new technological breakthroughs will be commercialized that will adversely affect the market acceptance forecast by this plan.

7. There is a 70 percent probability that no new legislation will be passed that will adversely affect manufacturing or marketing operations under this plan.

The magic question: How? The consultative salesman's presentation of his profit improvement objectives has one purpose. It is to induce his account's key decision makers and influencers to ask him the magic question, "How?" This question is the customer's way of opening the sale. It signals the customer's interest in the salesman's promise of profit improvement, his acceptance of its desirability and feasibility, and his motivation to know how the salesman proposes to achieve them. Once the question has been asked, the salesman can begin to sell. Until it is asked, the salesman is merely negotiating for the privilege of selling without being able to engage in the selling act itself.

STRATEGIES

Customer question they answer:
How are you going to add to my profit?
Assurance they give:
By applying a planned, progressive series of profit improvement projects to key aspects of your business.

In common with objectives, strategies also come in two types. The second set of strategies underlies the first.

The plan's *customer applications strategies* are the mix of the salesman's products and services, along with his own personal expertise, that he applies to his customer's business. They are the parts of his profit improvement projects that the customer sees and is concerned about. The second strategy set, the plan's *internal implementation strategies,* must take place inside the salesman's company. Sometimes, one or more of them will have to be instituted within the salesman's customer company as well. In either case, they provide the capability base from which the customer application strategies can be derived.

Internal implementation strategies are therefore actually assumptions which underlie customer applications. The bet the salesman makes with his management about them can be translated in this manner: Give me enough money to build this capability and I will return such-and-such a yield as a result. Some examples of these internal bets are as follows:

- Invest $x to reduce our cost of electron beam welding by developing our own in-house capability or negotiate more economical vendor prices.
- Invest $x to develop new high-temperature alloys with improved deflection.
- Invest $x to create our own production capability for enameled resistance wire.
- Invest $x to replace or upgrade obsolete and noncompetitive molding equipment.
- Invest $x to install an internal automated raw materials handling system.

Customer applications strategies are the action elements of the consultative salesman's miniplan that make a direct impact on his accounts in the form of profit improvement projects. In creating his strategy mix of customer actions, the salesman will find it helpful to test each strategy recommendation against six criteria.

1. Strategies should be derived from market need. To avoid overengineering or incorrectly engineering a plan, all strategies should have their genesis in meeting user requirements in the customer's markets. In this way, the salesman's planning process starts and remains market-oriented.

2. Strategies should be realistic. They should be based on genuine capabilities within the salesman's company or capabilities which can dependably be employed from supplementary suppliers. Strategies based on yet-unproven technologies should be avoided. By applying realism in his strategy selection, the salesman helps underwrite their effectiveness. When this criterion is combined with the concept of the minimix, strategies have the best chance of being both effective and cost effective.

3. Strategies should represent a minimix. They should add up to only the minimal number that can accomplish their objective. No more strategies than necessary should be recommended. But altogether, they must be sufficient to do the job. Since strategies are costs, every strategy makes a contribution to the investment base of the salesman's profit improvement plans. If the investment base becomes excessive, the salesman's plans may contribute to loss instead of profit. Minimizing the strategy mix is a strenuous test of the salesman's business management skills.

4. Strategies should be systematized. They should be built up from individual products and services into systems that provide multiple benefits in a closely interrelated, highly correlated manner. Few of the customer problems which the consultative salesman tries to solve will be one-dimensional. They will probably have more than one cause. Accordingly, they will almost certainly require multiple strategies for their solution. A system is a package of strategies which have a common objective and whose overall effect should be greater than any of its individual components.

5. Strategies should be controllable. Insofar as possible, their operation should be subject to monitoring and their contribution should be measurable.

6. Strategies should be in compliance with all legal constraints which affect them. They should also harmonize with policy and ethical considerations held by the salesman's own company, his key account, and his account's key customers.

Strategy systems

A strategy system of profit improvement projects is really a scenario which the consultative salesman produces as a problem-solving narrative for a key account. The strategy system tells a story. The shorter the story, the better. To paraphrase a consultative salesman's recital of his strategy scenario, what he is actually saying to his customer is something like this:

These are the processes in your business whose profit I want to improve. Here is the system of strategies I have put together to affect them in the smallest way possible to achieve the greatest results. Taken together, these strategies should be the most cost-effective means of achieving the profit improvement objectives I have promised you. For this reason, I call them profit improvement projects.

A consultative salesman for an environmental protection company puts together systems of profit improvement projects which are based on problem definition and evaluation services, construction and engineering of control facilities to solve the problem, financing the facilities in whole or in part, maintenance and operating services for the facilities, educational services to train the facility staffs, community public relations services, and informational services to keep the customer's management fully knowledgeable about environmental compliance codes and legislation that can affect its existing or contemplated processes.

A consultative salesman for a fire protection company puts together systems of profit improvement projects based on problem analysis, a plant and office design consultation service to engineer out as much risk as possible beforehand, equipment prescription and placement, and personnel training services in fire-fighting and in equipment maintenance and repair. Other companies provide total distribution systems, total money management systems, and other systematic approaches to problem solving which can improve their customers' profit.

The grandfather of systems selling is probably IBM, which defines one aspect of its business as improving the profit of its customers' office productivity. The process it concentrates on is word processing. The problem it seeks to solve is "the rising cost of handling an ever increasing volume of necessary paperwork." The system it provides is a "total communications system" as an alternate approach to "an individual typewriter here, an individual dictating machine there, a copying machine somewhere else."

Systems strategies help IBM sell office hardware. They also help IBM in another way. The problem-solving services, applications services, maintenance services, and other service components of IBM's systems mix help the company gain and hold secure footholds with its key accounts. There are four basic strategies which enable IBM and other systems sellers to operate successfully.

1. *Segment* your customers. Target the 20 percent of all accounts who are or who can be your heavy profit contributors.

2. *Seek out* the most important needs that customers express as problems. Get deeply involved with their processes where these problems occur so that you can acquire the knowledge to help solve them in ways that will improve profits.

3. *Sell solutions* to customer problems which are composed of systems of your products, their associated services, your company's support capabilities, and your own personal applications expertise.

4. *Structure service systems* from three types of professional services, including (a) maintenance, repair, and replacement services that keep you involved with your customers on a continuing basis; (b) educational services that teach customers how to maximize the benefits of your system and enable them to upgrade their ability to solve the kind of problems you are expert in so they can use more sophisticated systems from you; and (c) profit improvement services that provide the ultimate reward to your customers for doing business with you.

The razor-and-blades strategy. Many successful strategy systems for profit improvement are built around the concept of the razor and blades. The razor is a supplier's hardware. Product-oriented suppliers believe that their sales function is to sell hardware. Market-oriented suppliers, on the other hand, realize that their essential unit of sale is the blades. While the razor is a one-time or occasional purchase, selling the blades provides a source of repeat income. Furthermore, selling the blades gives a supplier's salesmen the opportunity to become consultatively involved in their customers' "shaving" process. It furnishes them with a reason to make frequent servicing calls on their customers in order to replenish the supply of blades, maintain the condition of the razor and perhaps repair or replace it, teach "shaving," and learn more about customer needs for "better shaves" and other closely related activities which can offer logical markets for new sales. In this way, a supplier can discover how to provide educational services which can insure the ongoing use of his razors and blades, seek out opportunities for new and improved products, and expand his service system into products and services which can profitably extend his existing business. Each new element of his learning process opens up new opportunities for profit improvement projects.

The most important advantage of emphasizing a systems approach to shaving, however, is simply this: It forces a supplier to focus on the combined effect of the razor-and-blade system and to express it in the same way a customer does, as his ultimate benefit. Systems selling focuses a sales approach on benefits as no other strategy can. As a result, Gillette is able to sell the ultimate benefit of shaving, good grooming, which solves the problem of how a man can look his best. Kodak makes the designs for its cameras available to competitors but it will not license another company to make the cameras' "blades," its film. Yet Kodak does not sell the film as film. It sells entertainment and self-enhancement as the film's ultimate benefit.

The consultative salesman's task in creating a profit improvement system is therefore twofold. First, he must tie in the blades with the razor. Second, he must sell the blades and not the razor by concentrating on how they profit their user and deliver the ultimate reward he seeks.

New product and new business planning

Two of the most important strategies which a consultative salesman can use to embed himself in a customer's marketing process are new product planning and new business planning. These strategies deserve special mention because they combine the probability of high risk with the possibility of high reward in terms of profit improvement for both the salesman and his customer.

New product planning. If a consultative salesman can help a key-account customer create, develop, and market a new product, he has a unique opportunity to make a sizable contribution to the customer's profit improvement. He will also be able to contribute to his own company's new profits. In addition, he will have a partnership share in the new product's information bank. He should therefore be able to put a lock on his continuing involvement as a supplier throughout the product's life cycle.

Creating concepts for new products and then helping in their testing and evaluation are the major ways open to the salesman in working on new products with his accounts. Figure 3.14 describes a three-phase method of new product and service concept development. It proceeds from basic market segmentation information on heavy-user needs to the creation and testing of product and service concepts designed to satisfy these needs. The salesman's payoff to the process is his recommendation for market planning action to bring acceptable concepts to the actual product prototype stage and to market testing.

The consultative salesman must accept the responsibility for producing a continuing supply of new concepts for this type of testing. He must then be able to work with his customer's product development and market research staff, together with the people and resources of his own company's industry information center, to help validate his concepts. Often, he will find himself coming up with new ideas that he will want to test, or to have tested, quickly and at relatively low cost. In such cases he will be greatly aided by his knowledge of how the physical characteristics that compose a concept, along with their user benefits, can be evaluated. One basic form of market validation is illustrated by the sample section of a concept research test in Figure 3.15.

New business planning. An evolutionary step beyond new product planning into even greater risk and reward is for the salesman to help a key account enter a new business opportunity. As the consultative salesman gains proficiency in market segmentation based on needs analysis, and in the creation of new product concepts that can serve a market segment's needs, he can apply his capability to his customer's new business venture activities. Customer venture teams exist in many companies to help seek out profitable new businesses which can meet the next generation of market needs. The salesman can help in their profit improvement.

Figure 3.14 A three-phase method of new product concept development.

PHASE I: INFORMATION

Market Information Search and Analysis

Purpose: To segment a market according to its perceived needs and according to its assignment of assets and liabilities to benefit values currently available to serve its needs; and to set potential boundaries for market acceptance of new benefit concepts, together with a preliminary profitability projection for each concept.

Methods: (A) Surveys of basic market information data available through secondary sources and data banks; plus

(B) Primary need-seeking market research.

PHASE II: CONCEPTS

Concept Generation

Purpose: To develop new product–service systems and new promotional benefit concepts, ranging from near-in concepts that are marginally renovative through far-out concepts that are radically innovative.

Concept Formulation and Testing

Purpose: To pretest market acceptance for benefit concepts and for their individual components, such as form, shape, size, color, texture, taste, aroma, ingredient values, packaging, price, distribution, brand naming and promotional theming, and service systems.

Methods: (A) In-depth group session interviews to define testing techniques and to determine the best communication of benefit concepts; plus

(B) Concept research, through either personal interviews or direct mail; plus

(C) Concept advertising, through either personal interviews or direct mail.

PHASE III: DIRECTION

Market Planning Action Recommendations

Purpose: To determine go, no-go decisions for each new concept per market segment.

Methods: An outlined market plan for each recommended go concept and suggestions for new approaches to market segmentation and benefit conceptualization for no-go concepts.

Reproduced through the courtesy of The Concept Testing Institute.

Headed by a venture manager, venture teams are generally composed of three talent resources: a *technical* resource who provides new product and new process development expertise; a *financial* resource who provides cost-price analyses of new venture business possibilities and who forecasts profit potential for them; and *marketing* resources in the form of product management representatives, sales representatives, and market researchers. Figure 3.16 indicates how a consultative salesman can integrate his new business development capabilities with a customer's venture team. His role can be twofold, both as an external contributor of his own expertise and as manager of his company's support services.

Figure 3.15   Concept research for a new product.

A New Measuring Device for Melting and Smelting Processing Operations					
Measuring Device Characteristics		*Importance*			
Easily portable: can be carried in one hand from test to test	−2	−1	0	+1	+2
Reusable: can be used for unlimited number of tests	−2	−1	0	+1	+2
Quick-disconnect: takes only 5 seconds to plug in or out	−2	−1	0	+1	+2
Multiple-purpose: can also be equipped to take samples	−2	−1	0	+1	+2
Computerized: readings can be automatically recorded and evaluated by computer	−2	−1	0	+1	+2
Single-source sales: measuring device, sampling attachment, and computer system are offered by a single supplier	−2	−1	0	+1	+2
Economical: the basic measuring device itself will sell for $30–$40	−2	−1	0	+1	+2

Reproduced through the courtesy of The Concept Testing Institute.

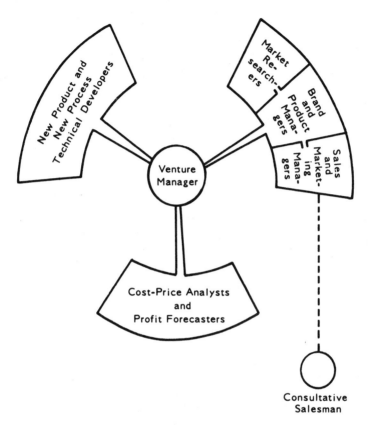

Figure 3.16   Integration of consultative salesman with new
business venture team.

Consultative pricing strategy

Consultative selling is an alternative strategy to selling on
price. Since he is offering significant added values, the salesman
who sells consultatively can forsake the option of being the lowest
price supplier. Nor will he generally need to be a parity pricer.
Consultative selling is designed to allow a company to be the
high-priced supplier in its field because high price validates the
salesman's claim of added value.

Consultative pricing strategy demands that the salesman

ask himself the question, "How much?" rather than "How little?" when he makes his pricing decision for each strategy system. Since he will already have designed his system around the smallest number of components rather than the largest, his combined system and price question can be expressed as, "How small a system can I sell at how high a price?"

By setting a high price for his own personal services as well as his product and service systems, the consultative salesman is doing more than simply recapturing the added cost of the values he represents. He is putting himself under the "consultant's pressure" to deliver. His customers can justify paying a higher than market price once on the anticipation of receiving unusual returns on their investment. But they will pay the salesman's price a second time only if they perceive his price-value relationship is in their favor. This means that customers must feel they are getting even more than they pay for in terms of the salesman's consultative services and the ability of his product and service systems to improve their profit.

Because the consultative salesman's price endorses his added value, he must overcome the salesman's traditional reluctance to face the price problem. Instead of being embarrassed about charging the customer, or defensive about customer reactions, the consultative salesman can use price to place an umbrella of value over his presentations. He will very often put his umbrella up first, right at the beginning of his presentation, instead of tucking it away until the end. This approach has important advantages. It imputes value. It alerts the customer to expect value and conditions him to relate each individual value to the salesman's total system. It frees the salesman from price dread. It allows him to devote the major part of his presentation to constructive description and interpretation of his plan. And it distinguishes him clearly from the product salesman who waits until the end of his pitch to pop the price and who may then find himself beginning a second presentation entitled "Overcoming Price Objections."

Consultative pricing strategy has no immunity from objections. The consultative salesman will encounter price resistance under several predictable circumstances. If he has incorrectly perceived a customer's needs and has built his strategy system around them, he will be overpriced in relation to his value. If he has engineered his system beyond the customer's needs, he will be overpriced. If he has failed to create a climate of confidence with his customer, his price may be called too high when it is actually the customer's acceptance that is too low.

Some customers may react to price objection by desystematizing the salesman's strategy system, seeking to identify the contributory cost of each individual component. Their objective is usually to force a reduction in the cost of the least competitive component. Failing that, they may threaten to purchase it separately from an alternate supplier. To safeguard themselves, some salesmen refuse to desystematize. Others add a sufficient premium to each component so that whatever they lose in one place they make up in another. Calculating the margin of premium price can be crucial. If the premium is not perceived as excessive, it can still be acceptable as proof of added value.

When the hardware component of a salesman's system is new, exclusive, or sophisticated, it is least likely to be desystematized. As the hardware matures into commodity status, it becomes more and more exposed to price competitors. At that point, the added value of the salesman's consultative services remains his sole price support. In the last analysis, therefore, it is his services that permit his consultative pricing strategy.

For the salesman who is accustomed to regard high price as a burden, consultative selling's pricing strategy shifts the burden from defending a price premium to aggressively promoting a premium value in the form of profit improvement. Unselling price is no longer the problem. Selling profit improvement becomes the salesman's dominant benefit. Under its impact, initial cost is a subordinate consideration to the added value which it contributes. The salesman's question turns from "Will you pay my *price?*" to "Do you want my *added value?*"

Consultative selling allows the salesman to emphasize his objective of improved profit rather than the immediate higher cost of one or more of its strategies.

As long as the benefit of achieving the objective exceeds

the cost of its strategy mix, and as long as the benefit's value is sufficiently greater than competitive benefits, the trade-off can be a marketable one.

Time and budget frames

No profit improvement plan goes anywhere without a budget. Since time is money, and since money has no value unless it is correlated with time, the consultative salesman must position his plan within a time and budget frame. A plan's clock runs from the moment it is commissioned until its promised completion date. The budget's clock runs over the same course. At the outset, the salesman has 100 percent of his time and dollar budgets. With every day, a unit of time expires. Wit hevery strategy expenditure, a dollar unit becomes transformed into a potential investment or a loss.

The miniplan is therefore a combination clock and cash register. If the clock or the cash runs out before the plan has brought its objectives home, it has failed. To be on budget and according to plan also means to be on time.

In the back of the plan's cash drawer the salesman will be wise to put aside a 10 percent margin of dollars. He will also be wise to set the plan's clock ahead by the same amount. In both cases, he will be protecting himself against contingencies which may arise if any of the negative assumptions in his plan come into play.

CONTROLS AND CONTINGENCIES

Customer question they answer:

How can I be sure you're taking my business to the added profit you promised?

Assurance they give:

I'll prove it to you every important step of the way.

The consultative salesman's long-term ability to maintain a relationship that is profitable to his own company and his key accounts depends on creating a climate of confidence for their work together. Confidence is his ticket to continuity. With continuity, he should be able to generate added confidence on the basis of his repeated performance. This one-to-one interaction between confidence and continuity is the cement that binds a consultative partnership and immunizes it against competitive inroads.

To get into a key-account relationship in the first place, a salesman must deal from the strongest card he can hold from a position outside the account. This card is his information resource. But in order to earn the right to stay in—that is, the right to continue to build confidence—the salesman must surround his promise of performance with controls. Information gets him into a key-account relationship; controls help keep him there.

Three needs converge on a consultative salesman that require him to apply controls against his strategies. He must guard against catastrophic failure of his profit improvement plan by providing an early warning system that allows him to deal with problems in his plan's operations as soon as they occur and while they are still small. He must have a method of proving that his profit improvement plan is actually improving his customer's profit. And he must prove he has the ability to deal with problems by having contingency strategies on the shelf in case his original strategies go astray.

A monitoring system and a measurement schedule must therefore become integral parts of a consultative salesman's miniplan. He will have to set up periodic monitoring probes of main events in his plan such as the times when his profit projects are being launched or should be taking effect. The purpose of the probes is to permit the salesman and his customer to say one of two things as they move along together toward their profit improvement objectives. Either everything is going according to plan or something is off plan. In an off-plan situation, one of three decisions will have to be made: to do nothing, to take remedial action in the form of a previously planned contingency strategy, or to raise a red flag warning that a serious unforeseen situation is occurring which can threaten achievement of the plan's objectives.

A variety of monitors are available for the salesman to deploy. The signals which will come from his own information center are one major source. Confirming or denying signs can also be monitored from his customer's sales force, from dealers and distributors, from competitive reaction, and from trade or industry sources. Quick, inexpensive market research probes can also play an important monitoring role by contributing periodic measurements of key-customer and key-prospect attitudes and intentions. Measurements of sales statistics, share-of-market figures, and profit margins allow the salesman to feed new factual inputs into his planning process that can contribute importantly to his next cycle of profit improvement projects.

Controls expressed as measurements, monitors, and contingencies play several crucial roles in the consultative relationship. First of all, they help to insure the salesman and his customer against surprise. They also insure each of them against the other. Controls legislate joint performance and shared responsibility. Since these are the essential ingredients of partnership, it can be said that controls are the *planning tools* that allow a partnership to take place between the salesman and his customer.

Until controls are set up, no partnership can occur. No true trust can prevail. Without the fail-safe guidelines of control procedures, no commitment to go very far ahead, or for very long, can be made by either party. As onerous as controls may be, there can be no consultative selling relationship without them. They help guard the relationship against underachievement of its objectives. They also guard against overcommitment of either the salesman's resources or those of his customer. One of their greatest contributions, however, is to help prevent consultative selling from falling into the pursuit of inferior strategies which negate its promise.

Another major contribution which the plan's controls make to a consultative partnership is through the medium of the salesman's information resources. Controls feed back priceless information about the effectiveness of the salesman's strategies. As each measurement is made of progress in achieving his plan's objectives, the information brought in by the plan's controls becomes a part of the salesman's ongoing situation survey. In this way, his knowledge of the situation is kept up to date by reflecting the real world of the marketplace.

Since it is the salesman's information resources which make up his ticket of admission into a consultative relationship, the process of keeping it current can be regarded as one of its costs of maintenance. The application of control information to the situation survey's "knowledge box" illustrates the closed-loop concept of the consultative miniplan. Controls feed in new knowledge of the situation. With the situation's new information in hand, new objectives can be set and new strategies can be devised to achieve them. Once they are in operation, the controls then feed in even newer knowledge and the loop is repeated.

The sum total of traveling this information replenishment loop again and again is called *experience*. An experienced salesman has been around the loop many times. Each time he shares his information resource with a customer, and each time he refines it and renovates it with new knowledge from his controls, he strengthens the basis for his partnership. His information supply thereby emerges as the consultative salesman's most precious resource: his original entry pass into the relationship, the generator of his objectives and source of his strategy mix, and, along with his controls, the builder of his partnership.

4/Profit Improvement Strategies

For both the consultative salesman and his customers, profit is the name of the game. While the game is the same, the role the salesman plays in it is very different from that of his customer.

Setting profit objectives is the customer's business. It cannot be abdicated, nor can the customer delegate it to anyone outside his company. No one who is external to a company can ever know enough about corporate assets and liabilities—financial, operational, or human—to set the kind of overall business objectives that must be based on them. Besides, a consultant's concern with his customer's business is rarely an overall one. In the case of the consultative salesman, it is concentrated on the product and service systems, and their market segments, with which he himself is involved. As a result, the salesman's role is concerned with the additive effects his product and service systems can have on his customer's profitability.

A customer's primary management function is to develop strategic and tactical plans that can achieve profit maximization. The consultative salesman's role is limited to profit improvement. This means that the consultative salesman begins to plan his profit contribution from the point at which his customer has finished developing his profit plan. The end point of his customer's profit objectives becomes the consultative salesman's point of departure.

Taking off from his customer's planned level of profitability, the salesman's objectives specify the additive percentages of improvement over the forthcoming one to three or five years with which the consultative salesman can reasonably expect to supplement his customer's income.

As a profit improver, the consultative salesman will have to become a supplier of new income opportunities for each of his customers. As he approaches a customer's business with the objective of adding to the profitability of its operations, he will be aided by understanding the financial process of a business and how its profits are made. This will enable him to identify problems and opportunities for profit improvement. He must also be able to put together the fact base he will require in order to generate a consecutive chain of profit improvement projects.

PRINCIPLES OF PROFIT IMPROVEMENT

The substance of a customer's business is represented by its assets. Assets are composed of tangible and intangible resources. Tangible assets are resources that have physical character. Land, buildings, machinery, and inventories of various kinds are common examples. Intangible assets are resources that are financially real but have no physical character. Accounts and notes receivable, investments, and cash are all intangibles. Both tangible and intangible resources have economic values. The consultative salesman will find it useful to keep the dimension of these values in mind when he attempts to create new values through profit improvement. In this way, he will have a better idea of what he is adding to and how important his additions will appear to his customer.

HOW PROFITS ARE MADE

A customer uses the funds which are invested in his business, and which underlie its assets, as the foundation for profit making. Tangible and intangible resources are the basis of profits. This defines profits as the increase in resources during the operating cycle of a business.

Funds invested in the operations of a business are never static. They flow constantly. Because profit comes from this flow of funds, the consultative salesman must learn the nature of the flow, the kinds of business activities which influence it, and how the flow of funds can be tracked and recorded. He must also understand that the funds change form several times during a cycle of flow. Each time they change, the objective of business management is to increase them. The salesman's function is to contribute to this growth process by adding further to it. This enables him to become an integral part of his customer's profit-making system.

READING THE BALANCE SHEET

A balance sheet is a snapshot of a business that shows its financial condition at the moment in time when it is snapped. By learning how to read it, the consultative salesman can get an overall picture of the financial structure of a customer's business that will help him spot his best opportunities for profit improvement.

While balance sheets can take many forms, and the items which appear on them may vary according to the character of each business and its particular circumstances, a conventional balance sheet apears in part A of Figure 4.1. It contains five sections. Two of these sections appear on the left-hand or asset side of the statement: current assets and fixed assets. On the right-hand side three sections are found: current liabilities, long-term liabilities, and capital. It is important for the consultative salesman to know what each of these sections or categories includes and why, when the values assigned to the items on each side are totaled, a balance sheet must balance.

- *Current assets.* Cash as well as receivables and inventories that are expected to be liquidated into cash within one year.
- *Fixed assets.* The land, buildings, and equipment used in the operation of the business.
- *Current liabilities.* Accounts payable, short-term bank loans, current installments of long-term loans, bonds or mortgages payable, accrued payroll due employees, accrued taxes, and other amounts due to third parties within one year.

BALANCE SHEET

ASSETS	LIABILITIES
Current Assets	Current Liabilities
	Long-Term Liabilities
Fixed Assets	Capital (Capital Stock and Retained Earnings)

A

The balance sheet expressed as a statement of assets and liabilities.

BALANCE SHEET

FUNDS INVESTED	SOURCES OF FUNDS
Circulating Capital	Vendors Banks (Short-term)
	Banks Insurance Companies Bondholders (Long-term)
Facilities	Stockholders

B

The balance sheet expressed as a statement of funds invested and sources of funds.

Figure 4.1   The balance sheet.

- *Long-term liabilities.* Bonds, mortgages payable, and other loans due beyond one year.
- *Capital.* The value of a business to its owners. This value is called equity. It is created either by direct investment of funds in the business or by profits that are retained after payment of dividends to owners or stockholders. Since equity is determined by subtracting liabilities from assets, both sides of the balance sheet will balance.

The usual customer balance sheet must be translated by the consultative salesman into the form shown in Figure 4.1B in order to disclose the character of the underlying funds. In effect, part B is an x-ray of part A.

The left-hand side of Figure 4.1B represents the funds invested in the business operation of a customer. It shows at a particular point of time where and in what form these funds reside. Current assets are the funds invested in the circulating capital of the business. Funds invested in the facilities used to operate the business are fixed assets.

The right-hand side of Figure 4.1B shows the current sources of the funds which have been invested. From it, the salesman can determine the specific proportion of his customer's total invested funds that has been individually contributed by vendors and banks on a short-term basis, by banks, insurance companies, and bondholders on a long-term basis, and by the owners and stockholders as a result of direct investment or retained operating profits in excess of dividends paid out.

As a rule, management of the left-hand side of the balance sheet (representing the funds invested in a customer's operations) is the responsibility of his operating management. The right-hand side of the balance sheet, representing the sources of funds, is the responsibility of his financial management. Since the cost of acquiring and maintaining funds differs depending on their source, financial or money management is an important function contributing to profitability. A consultative salesman who deals in products and services related to financial or money management will want to pay particular attention to the balance sheet's competitive sources of funds. He may find the right-hand side of the balance sheet useful for determining how his products or services can reduce his customer's cost of acquisition or maintenance of funds and thereby contribute to the profitability of his business. On the other hand, a consultative salesman whose products or services affect the operations of his customer's business will be more interested in the funds invested in the operating assets of a customer business. Because credit terms affect the financial management function, they will be of interest to all consultative salesmen regardless of the products or services they sell.

THE INCOME STATEMENT

Increases or decreases in the value of a customer company's capital are generally the result of one or more of three conditions:

1. Capital value will increase if additional capital is obtained.
2. Capital value will decrease if dividends are paid out.
3. Capital value will increase if the net result of operations is a profit and will decrease if the net result of operations is a loss.

By far the most significant factor in determining capital value is the net result of operations or the earning power of the business. Therefore, this aspect of profit making is reported in a separate statement known as the income or profit and loss (P&L) statement. On it, profit appears as the remainder of revenues from which expenses have been subtracted. This statement of profit gives the consultative salesman the bench mark from which his profit improvement objectives must take off.

THE CIRCULATING CAPITAL PRINCIPLE

Profit is made by the circulation of business capital. Every business is founded on capital, or funds "originating" in the form of cash. The objective of business is to make its initial cash grow into more cash. The way this is accomplished is to circulate the capital or initial cash by flowing it through three transfer points, each one of which adds value to it:

1. The initial cash circulates first into *inventories*.
2. Then the inventories circulate into *receivables*.
3. The receivables finally circulate back into *cash,* completing their cycle.

This three-step process demonstrates the principle of circulating capital. Every business depends on it for its income.

Circulating capital is the current assets of a business. They go to work in profit making as soon as cash is invested in accumulating inventories. Every time raw materials are purchased or processed, inventories come into existence. Another name for production scheduling could really be inventory conversion. Manufacturing adds further to the values of inventories, and so do all the other processing functions of business that transfer value on a dollar-for-dollar basis from cash to product costs.

Figure 4.2 shows the profit-making process which occurs as capital funds circulate through a customer's business. In part A the funds are in the form of cash. As the business operates, the funds change form. The initial cash is transferred into inventories as the result of payment for raw materials, labor, and the manufacturing expenses of work-in-process and finished-goods inventories. In many cases, further expenses are incurred by changing the location of inventories from plant site to warehouse.

When sales occur, as in part B, funds then flow from inventories into receivables. As they flow, the magnitude of the funds increases since inventories are valued at cost and receivables are valued at selling price. This increase represents the gross profit on sales. The greater the gross profit rate, the greater the increase in the magnitude of funds during each rotation of the capital circulation cycle.

Figure 4.2C shows how the funds earned by the collection of receivables flow back once again into cash. Before they do, they are reduced in magnitude by the subtraction of the sales and administrative expenses which have been disbursed throughout the

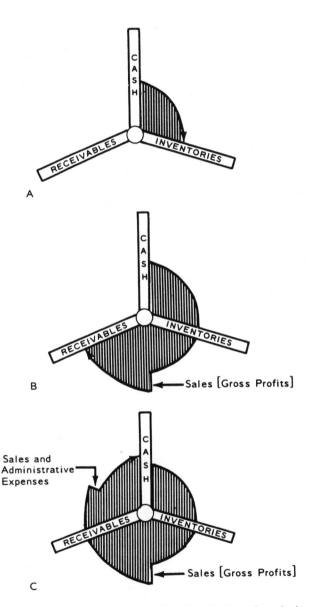

Figure 4.2   The profit-making circulation of capital.

operating cycle. At this point, one full cycle of capital circulation has ben completed. It has resulted in an increase in the number of dollars in the circulating capital fund. This increase is measured by the difference between gross profits and selling administration expenses. In other words, a profit has been made by turning over the circulating capital of the business one cycle. The more cycles through which the consultative salesman can help turn his customer's circulating capital during an operating year, the greater the profit he can help earn. This is the principle of turnover.

THE TURNOVER PRINCIPLE

The circulation of capital funds in a customer's business takes on meaning to the consultative salesman only when he relates it to a given time frame. Since capital funds turn over in a complete cycle from cash to inventories, to receivables, and then back into cash again, their rate of flow can be measured as the rate of turnover. The faster the turnover within any time frame, the greater the profit.

Stepping up his customer's turnover rate through profit improvement projects is the consultative salesman's most important function. Unless his profit projects are by and large directed to improving the turnover of the capital employed in his customer's business—especially the capital that is in the form of inventories—the consultative salesman cannot possibly accomplish his mission.

Turnover will generally offer more opportunities than any other strategy for profit improvement. The most common way to improve turnover rate is through increased sales volume and lowered operating fund requirements. In some situations, turnover may be improved by decreasing sales or even increasing the investment in operating assets. This can be accomplished by adopting a selective marketing strategy. Products or markets will have to be eliminated wherever the sales volume loss and associated funds invested indicate that the turnover rate is substantially lower than an average of all products or markets. There will then be a decrease in total sales, but a proportionately greater decrease in invested funds. Occasions also exist in which an increased investment in operating assets can yield a higher than average turn-over rate in selected product lines or market segments.

The consultative salesman is in an excellent position to help improve a customer's turn of circulating capital since, as Figure 4.3 shows, the drive wheel that rotates capital is sales. The salesman must continually search for the optimal relationship between his customer's sales volume and the investment in operating funds required to achieve it. At the point where the optimal relationship exists, the turnover rate will yield the best profit.

In the basic relationship between circulating capital, total capital employed, and sales shown in the figure, the circumference of the sales wheel represents $200,000 worth of sales during a 12-month operating period. The sales wheel drives a smaller wheel representing circulating capital. The circumference of the circulating wheel equals the amount of dollars invested in working funds. If sales are $200,000 per year, working capital will be $100,000. Enclosing the circulating capital wheel is a larger wheel which is also driven by sales. This wheel represents the total capital employed. It includes the circulating capital of $100,000 plus funds of $100,000 invested in plant and facilities. Thus the circumference of the wheel representing total capital employed is $200,000, equal to the sales drive wheel.

When annual sales are $200,000 and total capital employed in the operation is $200,000, then the annual turnover rate of funds invested is 100 percent or one turn per year. Circulating capital amounting to $100,000 of the total funds invested will turn over at the rate of 200 percent or twice a year.

Each of the elements of circulating capital—cash, receivables, and inventories—will have its own individual turnover rate. Inventory turnover is calculated according to the number of months' supply on hand. A six months' supply would represent two turns per year or a 200 percent annual turnover rate. Turnover of receivables is expressed as the number of days' business outstanding. If 90 days of business are outstanding, the receivables turnover is four turns per year or 400 percent.

With the basic relationships of Figure 4.3 in his mind, the consultative salesman can address the problem of helping his cus-

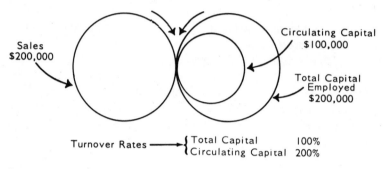

Turnover Rates ⟶ { Total Capital   100%
                 { Circulating Capital   200%

Basic Relationship

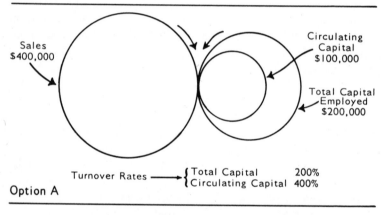

Turnover Rates ⟶ { Total Capital   200%
                 { Circulating Capital   400%

Option A

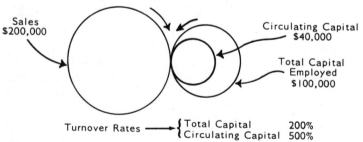

Turnover Rates ⟶ { Total Capital   200%
                 { Circulating Capital   500%

Option B

Figure 4.3   The turnover principle.

tomers achieve one of their most important objectives: maximizing the turnover rate. Since a customer's circulating capital increases every time it completes one turn, the salesman must find ways to contribute to increasing customer turnover by the use of his product and service systems. In this way he will be able to make his most significant profit improvement.

Fundamentally, a consultative salesman can exercise two options for improving turnover. One way, shown in option A, is by increasing sales. The other way is by decreasing the amount of funds invested in circulating capital, as illustrated in option B.

In option A the salesman has an opportunity to double his customer's sales to $400,000 per year without increasing the $200,000 of total funds employed in the business. The turnover rate will be increased this way from 100 to 200 percent. At the same time, the turnover rate of circulating capital increases from 200 to 400 percent. Option B demonstrates an alternative opportunity to improve turnover if the salesman cannot increase his customer's sales. If sales remain at the same annual rate of $200,000, turnover can be increased if total capital employed is reduced from $200,000 to $100,000. This includes a parallel reduction in circulating capital from $100,000 to $40,000. These reductions help the salesman improve the turnover rate of total capital employed from 100 to 200 percent and the turnover rate of circulating capital from 200 to 500 percent. This strategy for improving turnover means that the operating funds of the business are being worked harder.

The profit improvement created by options A and B can be readily appreciated by multiplying the increase in magnitude of funds generated at each turn of the operating cycle by an increasing number of turns. If the operating profit from one turn in the basic relationships shown in Figure 4.3 is $50,000, the profit realized by option A would be doubled to $100,000. In option B, profit would remain at $50,000 but $100,000 of funds would be released from operations that could be used to generate additional business or reduce indebtedness.

Opportunities abound for improving a customer's turnover performance. The reason is simple. The sum total of funds employed in a customer's business represents the many component funds that make up circulating and fixed capital. An improvement in the turnover of any one of these components will correspondingly improve the turnover of the total funds employed. Therefore, the consultative salesman may zero in on any component without the need to consider any of the others or their sum total. For example, improvement in the turnover of any single item in a customer's inventory—including the salesman's own products—will improve total turnover and consequently contribute to profit improvement.

THE RETURN-ON-INVESTMENT YARDSTICK

In order to tell whether sales performance under a profit improvement project is good or poor, the consultative salesman requires an accurate yardstick. In many selling organizations, profit is commonly expressed as a percentage of sales price or as an absolute amount per unit. But any method of measuring profit as a percentage of sales is insufficient for the consultative salesman's purposes since it takes into account only two elements of profit: sales value and cost. The difference between them is then calculated as a percentage of sales. Profit, however, has a very important third component: *time*.

From the point of view of return, profit can be regarded as the ratio of income earned during an operating cycle to the amount of capital invested to produce it. Thus profits have two costs: (1) time costs (the costs of invested funds required to create the business and keep it going) and (2) costs of producing the product or service. Either of these measures profit quantitatively. When profit is measured in this way, by comparing it with its funded investment, it is being expressed as a return on investment, or ROI.

Return on investment is an analytical tool that has three qualities in its favor for the consultative salesman's purposes: (1) It is a fair and equitable measurement of profit contribution; (2) it is helpful in directing attention to the most immediate profit opportunities, allowing them to be rank-ordered on a priority basis; and (3) it is likely to be readily understood and accepted

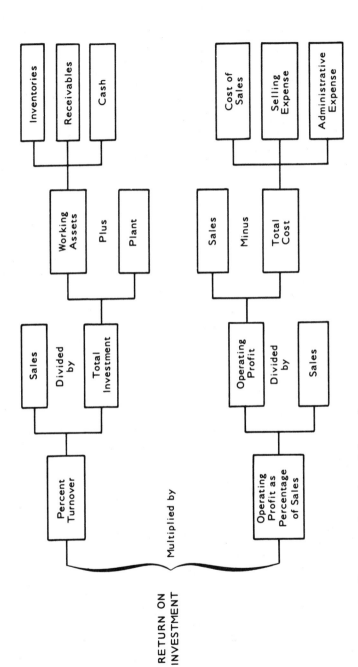

Figure 4.4   Return-on-investment formula.

by the financial managers as well as the sales and marketing managers of the salesman's customer companies.

Figure 4.4 represents the formula for calculating return on investment. The formula relates the major operating and financial factors required in profit making to the rate used to measure the profit that is made: the rate of profit per unit of sales in dollars, the rate of turnover of operating funds, the funds required to finance business operations, and the total investment of capital employed, including working assets, plants, and facilities.

Because his customers can never forget it, the consultative salesman must always bear in mind that the sole economic justification for investing in a profit improvement project is to earn a superior rate of return on the funds invested. This managerial truism must be interpreted in two ways. One is in terms of income gained, which should be maximized by the consultative salesman's recommended profit projects. The other is in terms of costs avoided in obtaining investment funds, costs of retaining such funds, and costs suffered by denying their use for alternative, potentially more profitable projects.

A simple example will illustrate the value of the return-on-investment yardstick in helping the salesman select one profit improvement project over another.

Under project A, sales are forecast at $200,000 with the investment of $100,000 of capital. Profit is predicted to reach $20,000. Under project B, sales are forecast at $300,000 with the investment of the same $100,000 of capital. Profit is predicted to reach $30,000. On the face of it, project B looks like the better bet. Selecting one over the other, however, is made more rational by calculating profit as a percentage of sales and of capital employed:

>*Percentage of sales:*
>Project A: $20,000/$200,000 = 10%
>Project B: $30,000/$300,000 = 10%
>*Percentage of capital employed:*
>Project A: $20,000/$100,000 = 20%
>Project B: $30,000/$100,000 = 30%

The two projects work out as equally worthwhile on the basis of their profit on sales. But in terms of the return each can bring back on the basis of the capital resources it employs, project B is superior.

The factor which accounts for the difference between the two projects is the relationship of their sales volumes to the capital employed. Project A allows its capital to turn over at the rate of 200 percent. In project B, however, the turnover is 300 percent.

Using the figures in the example, a simplified formula can be arrived at for the consultative salesman to use in making preliminary computations of the profit projects he may want to recommend.

$$\frac{\text{Profit}}{\text{Sales}} \times \frac{\text{Sales}}{\text{Capital employed}} = \text{Percent return on investment}$$

In the case of project A, the computation is:

$$\frac{20,000}{200,000} \times \frac{200,000}{100,000} = 20\%$$

In the case of project B, the computation is:

$$\frac{30,000}{300,000} \times \frac{300,000}{100,000} = 30\%$$

In this simplified approach, the first fraction helps the salesman calculate the percentage of profit he can expect on sales. The second fraction calculates the turnover rate. When the two fractions are multiplied, they determine return on investment. It is therefore easy to appreciate why turnover is regarded as the multiplier of profits. Any improvement in the turnover of funds invested in a profit project's total assets, working assets, or any component part of an individual asset will increase turnover and therefore have a multiplying effect on profits.

The simplified formula for ROI can be simplified even further for use as a quick screen by the consultative salesman who wants to make an early rule-out of profit projects which cannot offer superior potential. In such cases he can cancel out the sales figures in the formula and work with it in this ultimate condensed version:

$$\frac{\text{Profit}}{\text{Capital employed}} = \text{ROI}$$

However, the salesman should be careful not to use this stripped-down formula for anything more than preliminary quick screening purposes. Without the ability to disclose the significance of the costs and the level of capital employed in relation to sales volume, the salesman will be limiting his scope and accuracy in recommending profit improvement projects that can yield the best values.

RETURN-ON-INVESTMENT ADEQUACY

The consultative salesman's objective is to generate profit improvement opportunities for his customers that will deliver superior new income. In order to determine what "superior" means to his customers, he must first determine their concept of adequate return. The standards generally accepted as determining the adequacy of a rate of return are the basic cost of money, the risk associated with the operation of the business, and the return for technological capabilities. The consultative salesman can combine these concepts into a base rate of adequate return on investment, which is the lowest rate to exceed the following three considerations.

1. The consideration of the *basic cost of money* says that an adequate ROI must exceed the rate of return that can be realized for no-risk investments such as the interest rate on high-grade utility bonds or perhaps the prime bank interest rate. These rates set the floor of an adequate ROI and can easily be determined by inspection.

2. The consideration of the *risk* associated with the operation of the business says that an adequate ROI must acknowledge the odds for or against realizing the profits that have been forecast. The lower the risk, the lower the rate. The risk can be determined mathematically or subjectively.

3. The consideration of *return for technological capabilities* says that an adequate ROI must compensate for the long-term cumulative investment made in acquiring a profit project's income-producing capabilities residing in personnel, processing know-how, product design, patents, or business acumen. This investment factor can be determined mathematically and then given a subjectively weighted rate.

By keeping these three considerations in mind, the consultative salesman can help make certain that his definition of *adequacy* is the same as each customer's. This helps insure that his profit improvement projects will be able to meet their minimal needs. It will also help him avoid the embarrassment of recommending profit projects that are financially unacceptable and may therefore appear—along with him—to be irrelevant to his customer's purposes or even a frivolous appendage to them.

PERCEPTIVE PROFIT PLANNING

The fundamentals of profit planning are the same for the consultative salesman's customer as they are for him. The conditions under which they must be applied, however, are significantly different. The customer has access to his company's financial information resources, either in whole or in part. The salesman does not. The confidential data on which intensive financial analysis must be based will rarely, if ever, be made fully available to him. If it is, it will most likely be his reward for a lengthy period of successful consultation without them. For the most part, the consultative salesman will always have to cope with factual insufficiency.

It is therefore necessary for the consultative salesman to equip himself with a method of planning profits *perceptively* that he can operate from the very beginning of each customer relationship, even in advance of creating a climate of confidence. This method must be specifically tailored to serve his qualitative talents. Its major characteristic, however, and the one that fundamentally enables the consultative salesman to operate as a profit planner, must be an ability to make accurate financial diagnoses based solely on the kinds of information sources that are generally available to him. No certainty exists that the salesman's financial data bank can ever be significantly derived from inside information. His planning method for profit improvement must therefore be founded mostly on outside information. In other words, since his data cannot be customized, his method must be.

Perceptive profit planning is based on the fact that precise financial knowledge of a customer's operations is not essential in developing profit improvement opportunities. Very often, quantitative information may not be required either. As the consultative salesman becomes proficient in perceptive planning, he will be able to work more and more without the use of numbers at all. For example, he will find it can be sufficient to know that his customer's inventory level is substantially higher or lower than the industry average. He does not need to know by exactly how much in order to plan a profit improvement project around his knowledge.

THE WAY AROUND THE NUMBERS GAME

The consultative salesman's way around the numbers game is to work with reasonable assumptions whenever facts are insufficient. He can simply drop in numbers that will approximate the real figures. Most of the time he can come close enough to illustrate how profit improvement can be achieved. The key to working with assumed numbers is that they must be reasonably close to reality. And the key to being reasonably close is for the salesman to have an in-depth knowledge of his customer's business. This is another illustration of why the salesman's information is his most prized possession.

When a salesman's assumptions match the facts as his customer knows them, the salesman's recommendations will be received with more than average appreciation. On the other hand, if an assumption is erroneous but still reasonable, two eventualities can occur. The salesman's assumption can still suggest a solution to his customer. Or the customer may decide that such an unusually creative and perceptive fellow deserves to know the facts so that he can apply his wisdom against them.

THE PROFIT IMPROVEMENT INFORMATION BANK

The perceptive method of planning for profit improvement depends on two areas of knowledge: a selective knowledge of the customer's business and a broader knowledge of the industry and market in which it operates. These knowledge inputs should be deposited in each key account's profit improvement information bank so they can be withdrawn as they are needed to seek out and plan profit projects.

In his role as profit information banker, the consultative salesman must first of all be a selective *gatherer* of financial intelligence. Only then can he attempt to be a sophisticated *evaluator* of his data and a creative *recommender* of profit improvement projects based on his evaluations. But the second and third steps will be merely academic unless the first step is executed well. The salesman must know which facts and figures are truly pertinent to profit planning for a customer and where to find them in the public domain.

There are two main sources of profit improvement information: primary sources that originate information and secondary sources that collect primary data and then distribute it.

Primary information sources

Two of the most useful primary sources of the financial information required for a salesman's profit improvement planning are his customer's annual report and his periodic customer calls. If a company is not publicly held and no annual report is available, the salesman can fall back on his own company's credit information about the customer.

The annual report. The two essential sections of a customer's annual report are the president's letter and the descriptive text dealing with company operations. Ample financial data are usually available in annual reports to help the salesman prepare a simplified profit analysis. Two statements of financial information will be indispensable as major sources of pertinent facts and figures: the balance sheet and the income statement.

Customer calls. Every call should be regarded by the salesman as an information-gathering probe. The most effective method of gathering data from customer executives is through a consultative dialog with them that is centered around information related to the salesman's product and service systems. Perceptive data collection on customer calls should follow five principles:

1. Do not ask for any information that is obtainable from public sources.
2. Avoid asking for numbers.
3. Ask each executive only for the type and amount of information he can reasonably be expected to have. Do not ask a purchasing agent for financial information or the treasurer for purchasing data.
4. Ask only for necessary information.
5. Make notes of all gratuitous information even if there seems to be no immediate need for it.

Classification of primary information. The consultative salesman will find it helpful to classify the primary data he collects into three categories: (1) his customer's financial position, (2) profitability performance, and (3) cash and funds flow. Taken together, these categories will form an account's primary data bank for perceptive profit improvement planning.

Secondary information sources

A wide variety of secondary source material almost always exists to provide pertinent facts and figures about a customer's business. As Figure 4.5 shows, secondary sources are usually so prolific that the salesman's major problem will be selectivity. It is therefore extremely important for the salesman to know, before he looks, what he needs to know. The principles of profit planning will give him one of the best frames of reference for organizing his thinking before he begins his search and for coordinating it afterward.

By following the guidelines of the profit planning principles, the salesman can classify his needs for customer knowledge in the following sequential manner:

1. Assets and resources.
2. Sources of funds.

3. Significant financial ratios and trends.
4. Significant operating ratios and trends.
5. Identification of unrecorded resources.
6. Significant external economic influences.
7. Forecasts of trends or changes in external economic conditions.

Figure 4.5   Secondary sources of financial information.

A. U.S. Government
1. *Statistics of Income. Corporation Income Tax Returns. U.S. Business Tax Returns.* U.S. Department of the Treasury, Internal Revenue Service.
2. *Quarterly Financial Report for Manufacturing Corporations.* Federal Trade Commission and Securities and Exchange Commission.
3. *U.S. Industrial Outlook.* U.S. Department of Commerce Business and Defense Services Administration.

B. Business and Financial Publications, Subscription Services, and Associations
1. *Robert Morris Annual Statement Studies.* Robert Morris Associates.
2. *Dun & Bradstreet Key Business Ratios for 125 Lines of Business.* Dun & Bradstreet, Inc.
3. *Standard & Poor's Industry Surveys.* Standard & Poor's Corporation.
4. *Financial World.* Guenther Publishing Corporation.
5. *Forbes.* Forbes, Inc.
6. *Business Week.* McGraw-Hill Publications Company.
7. *Barron's.* Dow Jones & Company, Inc.
8. *Fortune.* Time Inc.
9. *Wall Street Transcript.* Wall Street Corporation.
10. *The Wall Street Journal.* Dow Jones & Company, Inc.

C. Industry and Company Reports Published by Individual Brokerage Houses. (Many of these are reproduced in the *Wall Street Transcript,* listed above.)

D. Industry Associations and Trade Publications Serving Individual Industries.

No matter how much homework the consultative salesman devotes to his primary and secondary source gathering, he will frequently be stopped dead in his tracks by the lack of some specific information. When this occurs he will have to turn to his own company's information resources or to market research. From these additional inputs he will be able to round out his knowledge and extend his grasp into otherwise inaccessible approaches to profit improvement planning.

PREDICTIVE ANALYSIS

The principles of profit improvement are the consultative salesman's major guidelines for predicting what can happen to his customer's profit under various approaches. By staying close to the guidelines, he will often be able to tell in advance the general outcome of his profit projects.

Even before he confronts his first set of fact and figures, the consultative salesman can put his experience or knowledge-by-observation to good use in predicting what will happen if a customer seizes a new profit opportunity. There are, for instance, certain types of businesses that the consultative salesman can predict from the beginning will suffer from inventory turnover problems. Any company that manufactures or stocks a large number of individual items can be considered a logical candidate for profit projects to reduce inventory investment requirements and thereby increase turnover.

Other businesses may have high investment requirements in receivables. The consultative salesman's plan for a reduction in this investment may lead to improved profit through an increase in the turnover rate of receivables. This, in turn, can improve the turnover rate of the total funds employed. In this way, the salesman can predict an improvement in the eventual rate of return on investment. On the other hand, companies in businesses such as food retailing already enjoy a high turnover rate. The salesman knows he can therefore predict that substantial income improvement will come from contributing only an extremely small increase in the profit rate.

The salesman's predictive process moves from establishing

a fact or making an assumption about a customer's business to basing a prediction on its implications. For example, the salesman may know or assume that the turnover rate of a key product in his customer's inventory is 4 times a year, or 400 percent. On this basis an average of three months' supply is kept on hand. When the salesman analyzes the rationale for maintaining this particular inventory level, he may learn that his customer's purpose is to provide superior market service. If his customer plans to increase sales of this key product by 50 percent, the salesman can predict that inventory will also have to be increased by 50 percent in the three-month period preceding the forecast sales increase.

The salesman's analysis of this sort of situation must also include a consideration of the source of additional funds that his customer will require in order to reach and maintain a higher inventory level. If the customer's assessment of future market demand is correct, the new funds will be generated by the additional profits arising from higher sales and greater turnover of his total funds. However, sales may not meet expectations. The salesman can then predict that the additional funds will have to come from a source other than planned in order to cover the investment in "slow-moving" inventory. Once again, this prediction can open up the salesman's thinking to supplementary profit improvement opportunities that can take up the customer's profit slack.

MINIMIZING THE FORECASTING ERRORS

The consultative salesman and his customer share an unreliable common bond when they sit down to plan profit: Each depends for his success on a forecast, which is a best guess as to what may happen. All plans begin with forecasts. Since there is no way to avoid them, the uncertainty that always surrounds forecasting must be lived with. The only certainty that can ever be made about a forecast is that, except by chance, it will be wrong.

Because being wrong is inevitable, the salesman must devote himself to minimizing the penalty for being wrong. The best way to avoid having a profit plan unduly penalized is to minimize the inevitable wrongness of forecasting by replacing the ignorance which underlies it with knowledge.

The sole knowledge that the salesman can bring to forecasting is the truism that a forecast can be wrong in only one of two directions: It can be too high or too low. Once the salesman accepts his fallibility and renounces attempts at clairvoyance, he can apply this knowledge to recommending profit improvement projects to his customers.

One of the most recurrent problems a consultative salesman faces is recommending the number of units of his product for a customer to buy in advance of a selling season and put into inventory. This decision must be based on the salesman's forecast of the market demand that he believes will be generated by his customer's customers. The only certain knowledge the salesman possesses is that the actual demand will be higher or lower than his forecast. But, as the following example shows, this is the only knowledge he will require.

OPTIONS FOR MAKING MINIMALLY WRONG FORECASTS

In Figure 4.6 two different industry situations are illustrated. In each, the salesman's options for minimizing the penalty of a wrong forecast are shown.

Part A represents an industry where short product life cycles are the rule. Procurement time is very often longer than the life span of market demand. The penalty for not having sufficient goods to sell can be catastrophic. The total contribution, or marginal income, of the product may be lost since no profit can be made on units that cannot be sold.

In working out his options for profit improvement projects with this type of customer, the salesman has drawn line AC in Figure 4.6A to represent his forecast level of demand. If the actual demand level is represented by line AB, the salesman has forecast too low and will incur a penalty. The area A-B-C in Figure 4.6A reveals the considerable scope of the penalty for forecasting too low.

The area A-C-D in Figure 4.6A shows the scope of the penalty if the salesman forecasts too high. The actual demand level as represented by line AD is now lower than the forecast. It is readily apparent that the penalties for forecasting too low and too

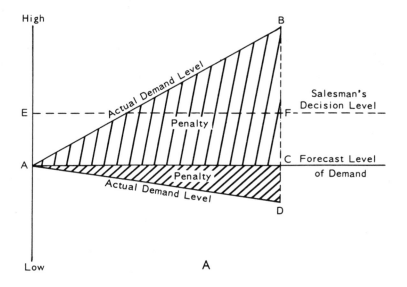

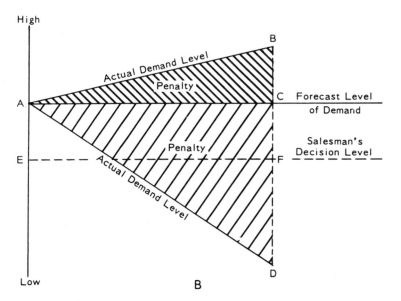

Figure 4.6   Minimizing forecasting error.

high in this industry are not equal. The salesman pays a higher penalty for forecasting low than he would pay for forecasting higher. To solve the problem of making a forecast that will be minimally wrong, the salesman must make the two penalties equal. Then, no matter what the actual demand level turns out to be, his degree of error will be minimal.

The line EF shows how the salesman can make the penalties equal whether the actual demand level is greater or lower than his forecast demand level. This line is called the salesman's decision level. He has placed it higher than his original forecast level at line AC, which carried with it an excessive penalty for being too low and inviting a stockout. By encouraging his customer to make a purchase from him at a level that could potentially represent overprocurement, the salesman is protecting the customer against the greater risk of profit loss by accepting the lesser risk of carrying inventory. In this way the salesman is fulfilling the role of improving his customer's profit. As long as the customer's product is not perishable, fashionable, or seasonal in nature, the penalty of paying an inventory holding cost, plus even a loss of the customer's funds which are frozen during warehousing, is still lower than the losses incurred from being unable to meet market demand.

Figure 4.6B shows another type of industry. Here the penalty from having product left over after a selling season is the total loss of its cost value. On the other hand, the penalty for overtime cost to make additional product is relatively small. Consequently, the salesman would put his customer into a reduced profit position when actual demand level proved to be lower than his forecast level of demand. To make the penalty for being too high equal the penalty for being too low, the salesman is encouraging his customer to underprocure as the best way to improve his profit.

DEBUNKING COUNTERPRODUCTIVE MYTHS

When the consultative salesman evaluates the comparative penalties that can be incurred in each customer's market situation, he will rarely need precise numbers. In many cases he will not require any numbers at all. What he will need, though, is the ability to question some of the most treasured myths of selling. One such myth says that shipping a product from one warehouse to another to meet unanticipated demand should be avoided at all costs. Even though it may be extremely expensive, transshipment between warehouses may represent a lower penalty than the cost of overloading all warehouses to avoid stockouts and transshipping charges. A good rule to follow is Heiser's law, which states: If there are no stockouts, the inventory is too high.

Another popular myth is that anything and everything should be done to avoid a lost sale. It is certainly true that nothing should be deliberately done that will invite the loss of sales. But there are many circumstances where losing a sale is less costly than making it or undertaking excessively costly corrective actions to try to save it. By concentrating on minimizing the penalties for being wrong, the consultative salesman can become alert to situations of this kind and confront the myths that can be counterproductive to improving his customer's profit.

GENERATING PROFIT IMPROVEMENT PROJECTS

A consultative salesman's day-to-day work is the generation of profit improvement projects, referred to as profit projects for short. Each project is a strategy to add value to his customer's profit objectives. The way the salesman adds value is through the application of his product and service systems and his own personal expertise to a small but meaningful part of the customer's business.

The process of generating profit projects must be a continuing one. Once it begins it can go on without end because the profit improvement opportunities in any customer company are limitless.

Profit projects are the components that make up the strategy section of the salesman's miniplan for his customer. They are the action elements that make the miniplan go. The value they add to the customer's business can be measured by the cumulative percentage of profit improvement they contribute. In Figure 4.7 a five-year cumulative profit of 60 percent is illustrated. This

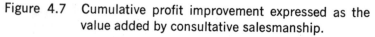

Figure 4.7 Cumulative profit improvement expressed as the value added by consultative salesmanship.

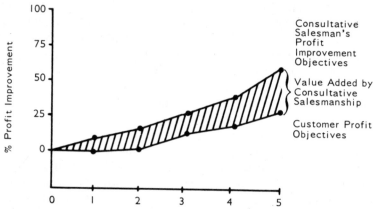

amount quantifies the salesman's contribution to customer profit over and above the profit objectives which his customer had already planned without the salesman's added value. In this sense, the consultative salesman positions himself as a profit-making strategy of his customer. If he can remain so, he can maintain himself in a long-term relationship.

THE MICROANALYSIS APPROACH

To be a customer is to be concerned with the total profit of a business. In analytical terms, this is a *macro* approach. A consultative salesman, however, is concerned with adding improvements in profit. His approach is to practice *microanalysis,* breaking down his customer's profit opportunities into relatively minute elements that he can get a handle on and affect in a positive manner.

As a microanalyst, the consultative salesman must develop a nose for the hidden causes of his customer's problems and the underlying reasons for his opportunities. He must think hard and think small. When he is confronted with an inventory problem, for example, it will not be sufficient for him simply to examine the problem as a whole or even in its larger parts. He must go to work microscopically to smoke out a profit improvement opportunity. He will probably have to consider the turnover rate of every single component in the affected product line, study each of them in the descending order of magnitude of their turnover rate, and find the specific product color, size, shape, price, or benefit that is the major contributing cause of the entire line's low turnover rate.

Microanalysis also prepares the salesman to begin to build his assumptions about what will or will not make a worthwhile profit project from the small details up rather than from an overall concept on down. If an improved share of market appears to be among the most promising approaches to a customer's improved profit, the consultative salesman must train himself where to start. One good starting point is the current number of product units sold by his customer as compared with the industry total. If a reduction in customer distribution costs seems likely to offer profit improvement advantages, the salesman must begin to develop information on how distribution costs compare with sales. From such finite calculations, infinite opportunities can be generated.

Isolated assumptions may also prove productive under microanalysis. The salesman may observe that his customer's inventory turnover appears slower than the industry norm. Nothing more than this notation may occur to him or even be visible. Nor may he have any information that inventory adjustment can exert any appreciable effect on customer profit. Nonetheless, the salesman's assumption that it could present a profit opportunity is enough to make him look further into it.

BUILDING PROJECTS AROUND CAUSES

As he carries out his microanalysis of a customer's operations, the salesman must dig out the causes of customer problems so that he can build profit projects to remedy them. To get at causes he must follow a three-step diagnostic procedure.

First, he will have to start from a *result*. If he were a doctor, a noteworthy result would be that a patient has abdominal pain. For the consultative salesman, a common result is that his customer shows a loss in an old, established product line.

Second, he will have to examine the result to find its *symptom*. The patient's symptom may be bleeding. The customer's symptom may be a major loss incurred in servicing a key account.

Third, he will have to probe beyond the symptom to identify its *cause*. The cause of the patient's bleeding may be a stomach ulcer. When the cause is removed, the symptom disappears and a different result can occur: the patient is now free of pain. The cause of the customer's loss may be the key account's extremely precise specifications that required the salesman's customer to purchase new manufacturing equipment and adopt unusually high-quality control standards.

The consultative salesman must get at causes if he is to generate successful profit projects. He will therefore have to practice a major precaution: to distinguish carefully between causes and symptoms, and never stop his diagnostic analysis with just the identification of a symptom.

Distinguishing between symptoms and causes is difficult because symptoms are more overt and usually easier to discover. They also call attention to themselves, often being identified by customers as "where we hurt." But they do not identify "why we hurt." Under microanalysis, symptoms are likely to become evident as the salesman studies the financial results of a customer's operations.

Identifying opportunities goes hand in hand with identifying causes of problems. Most of the consultative salesman's customers will probably be able to benefit by his ranking of their market segments according to a sliding scale of profit rate. It is imperative that the salesman's major cut at segmenting a business be made according to its customer groups. Only in this way can he help his customer maintain the market orientation of his business. Other segmental cuts can then be made according to product lines, sales territories, or salesmen. When that has been done, a matrix can be created to display the similarities and differences in profitability for each type of segmentation. Dissecting the most profitable segments may suggest multiple opportunities for profit improvement that can be applied by the consultative salesman to segments that are less profitable.

RETURN-ON-INVESTMENT DIAGNOSTIC TECHNIQUES

Diagnosis of his opportunities is always the salesman's major problem. It lies at the heart of consulting. In the beginning, the salesman must get his profit improvement show on the road by diagnosing an opportunity that will improve his customer's profit, deliver early visible results, and lead to another profit project. As he goes on, the criteria for generating successful profit projects multiply. His problem will not be simply that of diagnosing opportunity. It will also include testing solutions and evaluating probable benefits from his profit improvement recommendations.

The diagnostic techniques that offer the salesman the most legitimate promise of help are based upon the return-on-investment method of evaluating profitable performance. As Figure 4.4 shows, ROI is the product of the rate of operating profit as a percentage of sales and the rate of turnover. Any time the salesman wants to improve ROI, he must change either his customer's operating profit rate or his turnover.

Figure 4.8 illustrates the options open to a salesman for diagnosing profit opportunities that can improve turnover. He can, for example, recommend a project to reduce his customer's receivables. This will in turn reduce the amount of customer funds invested in working assets. And this will reduce the customer's total investment base. As a result, the salesman can improve his customer's profit without increasing his sales volume. Even though he may not have any numbers to put in each of the boxes of the

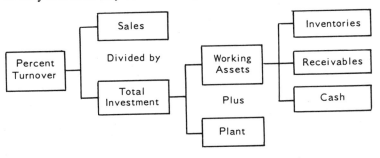

Figure 4.8   Options for improving turnover.

diagram, the salesman can perceive how profit improvement can be achieved. If numbers are required but are not available, the salesman can fill in the boxes with conservative assumptions about their real values and present them as his own perceptions, which are designed to approximate reality.

Figure 4.9 shows the options for diagnosing profit improvement if the salesman's objective is to improve operating profit. As an example, he can recommend a project to lower his customer's cost of sales. This will reduce the customer's total cost and thereby enable him to show an increase in his operating profit.

SEEKING SIMPLE OPPORTUNITIES

A salesman can find many relatively simple ways to recommend profit improvement. If he sells to supermarkets, he can show each chain's central headquarters or even individual store managers how substituting his brands for others, or increasing the number of their shelf facings, may improve profit per case or per $100 of sales. If the salesman sells to many small customers, he can develop an analysis of their major cost elements and use it to seek out with them their principal opportunities for profit improvement. Sometimes these opportunities will be found in excessive labor costs. Reducing this drain on profit may be best accomplished by substituting the salesman's equipment for the most expensive labor and then realigning the overall workforce. Or profit may be improved even more by stepping up volume.

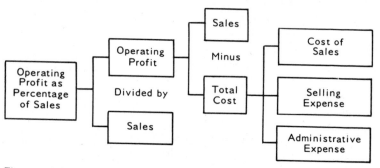

Figure 4.9 Options for improving operating profit.

A fertile area of profit improvement for most manufacturing companies lies in improving the profit of their dealers and distributors. By helping a customer's distributor organization to increase its contribution, the consultative salesman can help his customer to raise the profit on sales he makes through this channel, which he cannot directly control yet must nonetheless influence in his own self-interest.

A distributor's largest single investment is likely to be in inventory. The key to distributor inventory control lies in finding the minimum investment required to maintain adequate customer service. One way of measuring the utilization of inventory investment is to compare a distributor's inventory turnover with his industry's average. Industry turnover can be computed by using this formula:

$$\frac{\text{Cost of sales for one year}}{\text{Average inventory}} = \text{Inventory turnover}$$

If a customer's distributors are in a business whose inventory turns an average of 4.5 times a year, or once every 80 to 90 days, the salesman can help a distributor learn that his own turnover is lower than average by working out his projection in this way:

$$\frac{\text{Projected cost of sales}}{\substack{\text{Projected average} \\ \text{inventory level}}} = \frac{\$370,000}{\$100,000} = 3.7 \text{ Inventory turnover}$$

To help such a distributor increase his turnover to approach the 4.5 industry average, the salesman will have to help him reduce his investment in inventory. To do this, the salesman must first find out what level of inventory investment can yield a 4.5 turnover. This figure can be ascertained by dividing the distributor's projected cost of sales by the 4.5 desired turnover, which results in a $82,000 inventory. It now becomes clear that the salesman can help the distributor achieve profit improvement by controlling his inventory in such a way that his investment is reduced by $18,000, representing the difference between his current level of $100,000 and his desired level of $82,000.

The salesman's best approach to inventory reduction is usually through product line smoothing. The chances are high that distributors carry too many items in their lines. An inventory burdened by too many items can cause a dissipation of the distributor's sales management concentration, extra handling costs, waste through obsolescence or spoilage, and, of course, higher inventory carrying costs and overextended investment.

To analyze a distributor's inventory, the salesman can simply rank the products in his line according to their cost of sales volume and then compute their inventory turnover. Such an analysis could look like this:

Products A, B, C, and D account for 57% of the cost of sales volume but only 34% of inventory. These products turn over inventory by an average of 6.2 times a year.

Products E, F, G, H, J, and K account for 43% of the cost of sales volume but 66% of inventory. These products turn over inventory by an average of only 2.4 times a year.

The inventory turnover analysis in Figure 4.10 shows how the salesman can calculate what it costs the distributor to carry his projected inventory. By comparing the carrying costs of inventory to his forecast sales volume, the salesman can begin to learn

Figure 4.10 Inventory turnover analysis.

| Product | INVENTORY | | | | |
	% of Sales	Average $	% of Average	Turn-over	Carrying Cost as % of Sales
A	15	7,000	7	8.2	0.8
B	17	9,000	9	7.0	0.9
C	14	11,000	11	4.7	1.3
D	11	7,000	7	5.8	1.1
Subtotal	57	34,000	34	6.2	1.0
All Other Products	43	66,000	66	2.4	2.6
Total	100	100,000	100	3.7	1.7

more precisely what inventory the distributor should maintain. The first four products in the figure are apparently well controlled. They have a high average turnover rate of 6.2 percent and a low 1 percent average carrying cost as a percentage of sales. The salesman now knows that he must concentrate on reducing the distributor's inventory in his other products, whose average turnover rate is only 2.4 percent and average carrying cost is 2.6 as a percentage of sales. This will help him bring the distributor's inventory down to the $82,000 level which should contribute to his projected 4.5 inventory turnover.

PERCEPTIVE TREND ANALYSIS

If the consultative salesman can gather together information on the components that have made up his customer's turnover and operating profit over a time series of up to five years, he can search out profit improvement opportunities that are revealed by their trends. In this way he can see that sales may be increasing by x units or dollars each year. From this observation he can calculate the ratio of their increase year by year. He can also analyze the trend of the rate of increase to see if it is slowing, rising, or remaining the same. Rates of increase that are running down or appear stuck on a plateau may offer profit improvement opportunities.

Figure 4.11 shows the ratios which make up the return-on-investment formula. By plotting trends from year to year, the salesman can perceive targets of opportunity for the generation of profit projects. The figure contains customer operating information over a five-year period—in this case, actual data supplemented by secondary information sources. With equal effectiveness the salesman could have used reasonable assumptions based on his customer and industry knowledge.

Anyco, the company reflected in the figure, is a well-established custom manufacturer. Selling prices are traditionally set by adding a formula profit margin of 10 percent to estimated costs. The consultative salesman's diagnostic procedure, using trend analysis, follows a four-stage sequence: first, he makes *observa-*

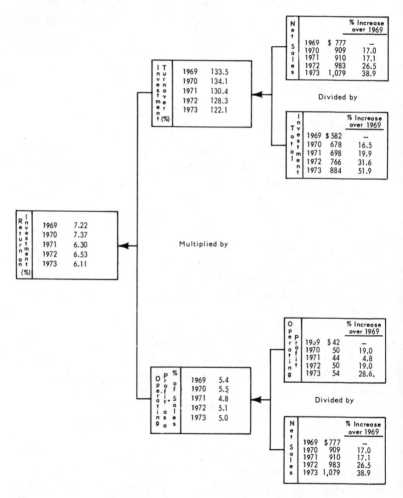

ANYCOMPANY
APPRAISAL OF OPERATING RESULTS
FIVE-YEAR COMPARISON
($000)

Figure 4.11   The ROI basis for generating profit improvement
                         projects.

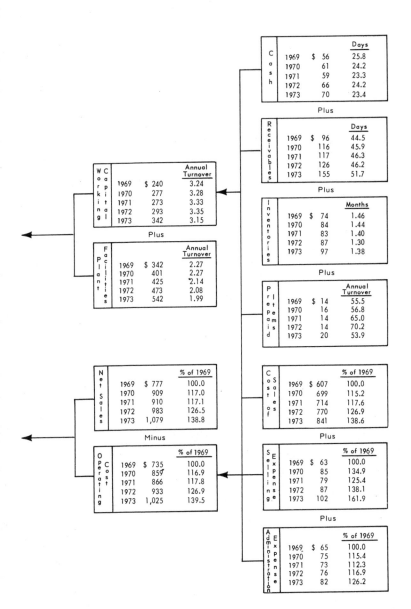

Figure 4.11   (continued)

tions supplemented by the distinction between causes and symptoms; then he creates a *hypothesis* based on his observations; next he makes a series of *inquiries* of his customer; and finally he creates an *assumption* about how he may be able to generate a worthwhile profit improvement project.

OBSERVATIONS

Anyco's return on investment shows a negative trend. During a five-year period it has declined from 7.22 to 6.11 percent. This ROI is dangerously close to the rate of interest that can be earned in no-risk investments. Since Anyco is not a no-risk venture, the company must find a way to raise its ROI.

The operating profit rate, a major component of ROI, has undergone a slight and perhaps insignificant decline from 5.4 to 5 percent.

The turnover rate, which is the multiplier of the operating rate, has significantly declined from 133.5 to 122.1 percent.

The two elements of the turnover rate, sales and total investment, have also increased. Sales show a fifth-year increase of 38.9 percent over the first year. Since an increase of this kind would normally improve the turnover rate, the even greater increase of 51.9 percent in total investment over the same five-year period has apparently cut it down. This, however, is a symptom and not a cause.

The investment in plant facilities shows a significant increase from $342,000 to $542,000, because automated manufacturing equipment was acquired as an offsetting response to rising labor costs. This is also a symptom and not a cause.

The acquisition of automated equipment has in fact reduced costs. Nevertheless, operating costs have increased 39.5 percent over the five-year period, paralleling the net sales increase of 38.8 percent. Hence the cost-price relationship shows little change.

HYPOTHESIS

Since only symptoms and no causes are revealed by the observations, the 5 percent operating profit figure may be due to slippage (1) between estimated costs and actual costs and (2) between estimated price and actual price. The cause may be poor estimating, or there may be some other reason for insufficient profit margin in establishing price.

SALESMAN'S INQUIRIES OF CUSTOMER

How do you arrive at your formula for calculating profit at 10 percent of estimated cost?

It's common industry practice.

Is the same formula applied to all your products, regardless of their cost per unit?

Yes.

Do you end up with a lower total unit cost for the products made on your automated equipment than on products still made by your manual operations?

Yes.

And is your price for these units therefore lower?

Yes.

Isn't it true, then, that the dollar amount of profit will be less on the products you make with your automated equipment?

It would appear so.

But since the acquisition of your automated equipment has forced you to make a significantly higher investment in operating equipment, shouldn't the amount of your profit on the automated units be greater—not less—to compensate for additional ROI required on the additional funds invested? Unless this happens, you are passing along to your customers all your cost savings, without recovery of a return on the additional investment in automated equipment.

That's very interesting.

Doesn't this lead to a hypothetical conclusion? You need to use at least dual profit rates in setting your sales prices so that there is one rate for manually produced products and another, higher rate for products manufactured on automatic equipment.

That's agreeable.

We can both figure out that to restore your ROI rate from the 6.11 percent where it is now to its best five-year level of 7.37

percent, you will need to gain 1.26 percent. If we assume your turnover rate will continue at approximately 125 percent, your operating profit rate will have to be increased by one percent. With no changes in your costs, your prices will have to average one percent higher. To take account of the inevitable slippage, your average mark-on should probably increase by 2 percent.

All right. We can see that. Now, how can you help us create the market acceptance that will assure us this profit improvement?

In this way, the magic question, *How?* has been developed by the salesman's perceptive trend analysis. He should now be prepared to answer it with a profit improvement project.

MANAGING A PROFIT IMPROVEMENT PORTFOLIO

The value of a consultative salesman's relationship with a key-account customer is simple to calculate. At any given time, it is the sum total of earnings from all the profit improvement projects his customer has invested in at the salesman's recommendation. A few will probably be spectacularly successful. But for the most part, steady modest success is all that is required.

Ideally, of course, each profit improvement project should be successful in its own right. Beyond that, it should also lead naturally into the next successful project. As his profit improvement contributions accumulate in a sausage-link chain, the salesman will be building an equity. His equity will consist of the value of the portfolio of profit improvement investments he has made in each account. The reward for good work will be more work. By inviting the salesman to remain in the game and try to improve profit one more time after each success, his customer is expressing a client's proper form of commendation. In a consultative relationship, the word "congratulations" is always followed by the phrase "you're vulnerable."

Along with all portfolio managers, the consultative salesman is only as good as his last investment. This should cause him to be financially conservative. Paradoxically, however, he will have to be creatively daring in conceiving profit improvement opportunities and planning to capture them. The net result of his union of these two characteristics becomes the essence of his personal managerial style as a consultant in improved profit.

STARTING SMALL

In setting about to construct a profit improvement portfolio, the consultative salesman should start small. At the outset he must be content to make a single profit improvement in one account. He should plan a project that is in a high-priority area of a key customer's business where profit improvement will be meaningful when it occurs. And since the project that comes first will probably be evaluated more critically than any of its successors, the salesman must follow one injunction above all others about his initial attempt to improve profit: *It must be successful.*

While all profit improvement projects should meet specific criteria, the first project must be sure to meet three standards in order to be judged successful: (1) It must add to the customer's profit rate (ROI) from an important product line or processing operation. (2) It must deliver early visible results that can be brought home as quickly as possible and are simply and agreeably measurable. (3) It must promise a logical carryover to an immediately following profit project and not result in a dead end.

TIME FRAME

To give his first profit improvement project every chance for success, the salesman should manage it on a more generous time frame than subsequent projects. An average second or third project will probably require a 90-day time frame from approval of its proposal through completion and evaluations. The first project, however, should be allowed double this amount.

A 180-day time frame for an opening profit project can be allocated in this way: The first period of 60 days is devoted to the salesman's homework and to educating his customer in what to expect. Unless this anticipation stage is properly set, it may be impossible to evaluate the project's results. Without expectations there can be no evaluation. Following the preparatory phase, 90 days for execution and 30 days for evaluation will run out the project's 180-day total time frame.

In year 1 of managing a profit improvement portfolio, the salesman· should therefore budget his first 180 days for project 1 and the remaining 180 days for projects 2 and 3. In year 2 he should be able to improve on his performance. On the basis of 90 days per profit project, his year 2 and subsequent profit improvement portfolios should include an average of four projects per year.

PROFIT IMPROVEMENT PROJECT CRITERIA

In selecting the ongoing investments he will make in his profit improvement portfolio, the consultative salesman will make his task easier if he follows a half dozen criteria. Their purpose is to steer him toward profit improvement projects that have the greatest chance of succeeding for him and his customer and the least chance of turning out to be merely exercises.

1. A profit improvement project should be achievable within an average 90-day time frame. Shorter projects risk trading off meaningful results for early accomplishment. Longer projects incur unpredictable risks. They not only defy ready calculation but invite cancellation or disenchantment.

2. A profit improvement project must offer the promise of achieving an addition to the customer's return on investment or avoiding a unique loss. The value it seeks to add should, in either case, be superior to the penalties which may threaten its achievement.

3. A profit improvement project should be profitable for both the consultative salesman and his customer. Shared profit improvement should not be confused with equal profit. The first objective—profitability for both—is a vital aspect of the concept of consultative selling. The second—equal profit—is rare over any short term of a consultative relationship and may be impossible to achieve no matter how long it endures.

4. A profit improvement project must draw on a major product or service capability of the salesman's company if it is to be profitable for him. Similarly, in order for his customer to profit, the project must affect one of his major products or services as well.

5. A profit improvement project's contribution must be measurable in terms of incremental net profit or decremental investment in operating assets. If it cannot be measured, or if no provision is made to quantify it, agreement on whether it even took place may be impossible to obtain.

6. A profit improvement project should not be an isolated entity in itself but should be a module which leads naturally to the next project and then to the next one after that.

THE PROFIT IMPROVEMENT PROJECT LOG

The consultative salesman's cumulative experience in planning the profit improvement of a number of key accounts is his trump card. He must have it up his sleeve and ready to play when his customers ask him, "What makes you think you can improve my profit from outside my company when I can't do it even though I work here?"

The salesman's best response is to refer to his track record and reply simply, "Because I have done it before under similar, or even more difficult, circumstances." To document his testimony the salesman should maintain a log of his profit improvement projects. The log should summarize the essential facts of each profit opportunity, the diagnostic procedures the salesman followed, the action strategies he recommended as a result, and their outcome. Unsuccessful projects should be logged along with the successful ones so that the salesman can learn not only what to do but what not to do again. This is vital educational material for him to teach his customers as well.

By cross-indexing his log according to types of opportunities, types of solutions, types of markets, types of products, and types of surrounding circumstances, the salesman will be able to relate his experiences most readily to current profit inprovement challenges.

As a result of his cumulative experience the consultative salesman's ultimate contribution to profit making may lie in his ability to use his log to focus attention on the rules for success in his customer's business. So much attention is normally focused on exploring failures that investigations of success are rare. Managements more readily vow not to repeat their mistakes than they pledge to learn from their successes. As a result, they find themselves unable to repeat them or reinstill their principles into new strategies. It is as often true in professional marketing management as in professional sports: When you lose, you can't let go of a game. You lie awake at night replaying it, trying to undo your mistakes. But when you win, it's another story. There's nothing to think about. The game is gone as soon as it's over.

As an external source of supply to his customer, the consultative salesman has an implicit need not to become more reactive to problems than creative of opportunities. Nor can he permit himself to be an analyst of failures more than of successes. It is inevitable that the consultative salesman will be called on time and again to help put out problem fires as they occur. But the major aspect of his role over the long run must be to spotlight business strategies that are historically and currently profitable for his customer and to instill this knowledge of success into the long-term growth of his customer's profits.

5/The Next Generation

As THE PRACTICE of consultative selling evolves it will offer a logical basis for some of the innovations that may characterize the next generation of sales management. Four of these innovations merit specific consideration: (1) the resident salesman, (2) the corporate "3-S" system of sales support services, (3) the sales college, and (4) the semiautonomous sales company which can be spun out of its parent corporation.

THE RESIDENT SALESMAN

The decade of the 1970s will undoubtedly require all businesses to segment their markets with stricter sophistication. If for no other reason than to control the ever rising cost of sales, supplier companies will have to segment their customers into at least two basic groups: (1) actual and potential high-profit heavy buyers and (2) all others. The actual and potential heavy buyers will rarely compose more than 20 or 30 percent of all customers, but they will account for perhaps 60 to 80 percent of all profitable sales. Because of their fundamental importance to a supplier, they will have to receive more than just top-level care. They may be required to receive *constant* care from a consultative salesman who will be in more or less continual residence within each heavy-buying customer company. Lower-profit, lighter, or more sporadic buyers will meanwhile continue to be served by the regular itinerant type of salesman calling on his normal transient schedule. The concepts that support the need for a resident salesman may be summarized in this way:

- The more scientifically managed a company is, the more market-oriented it will be and therefore the more strictly it will segment its markets.
- The more strictly a company segments its markets, the more it will concentrate its business on its high-profit, heavy-buying customers.
- The more concentration a company devotes to its high-profit heavy buyers, the smaller its market base will be and therefore the greater its risk of loss from the defection of any single customer.
- The smaller the market base and the greater the risk each customer loss represents to a company, the greater the need to insure against customer loss and to interweave customer growth with supplier company growth.
- The greater the need to insure against customer loss and harmonize customer-supplier growth, the more likely it becomes that the ideal coordinating agent will be the consultative salesman, that his ideal calling frequency will be daily, and that his ideal branch location will be in residence within his client company.

The resident salesman's presence inside the ongoing business organizations of one or more of his customers acknowledges their prime importance to his company. It also acknowledges the consultative salesman's importance. He will be a true medium, coordinating the two companies' long-term growth and development. As his knowledge and experience grow, the contribution he can make to his customers can grow too. It will not be unusual for him to occupy a place on his client's organization chart. The example in Figure 5.1 shows the consultative salesman occupying an "upstairs" office location for a packaging supplier who has installed can-making operations "downstairs" in a brewer's plant. This enables the brewer to save significantly on transportation,

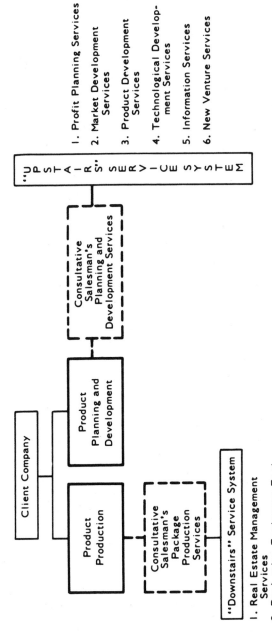

Figure 5.1 "Upstairs-downstairs coordination" by the consultative salesman.

Client Company

Product Planning and Development

Product Production

Consultative Salesman's Planning and Development Services

Consultative Salesman's Package Production Services

"UPSTAIRS" SERVICE SYSTEM

1. Profit Planning Services
2. Market Development Services
3. Product Development Services
4. Technological Development Services
5. Information Services
6. New Venture Services

"Downstairs" Service System

1. Real Estate Management Services
2. Production Equipment Engineering and Manufacturing Services
3. Production Personnel Recruitment and Motivation Services
4. Package Manufacturing Technology Services

storage, and handling costs and yet retain the benefits of the supplier's manufacturing technology and materials expertise.

In the figure the brewer owns the building that houses the canning facilities. The packaging supplier owns the production equipment, hires and controls the production personnel, and retains full responsibility for the can-manufacturing operations. "Downstairs," at the production level, the division of responsibilities is clear. "Upstairs," at the consultative salesman's level, the responsibilities are more thoroughly interwoven. By his position's very nature, the consultative salesman must be responsive to his customer's needs while being responsible to his own company. As the planning and administrative intermediary between them, his overriding interest is to improve the profit potential of their partnership.

For the packaging supplier, the consultative salesman in residence carries out a wide variety of functions. Simplest to perform is the determination of the number of cans his client-customer will be in the market for each year, their size and shape specifications, and their materials composition and delivery dates. In practice, these decisions will normally be the output of each annual manufacturing and marketing plan, which the consultative salesman and his customer's planning, development, and operating departments prepare in concert with each other. On a more consistent basis, the resident salesman's functions will probably involve most of the following planning and development services:

- Profit planning services.
- Market development services.
- Product development services.
- Technological development services.
- Information services.
- New business venture services.

It is easy to see why this combined upstairs-downstairs relationship, in which a supplier's production and consultative selling facilities are both locked into the heart of a key customer's business, has been referred to as "a major change in the historical relationship between supplier and customer." In itself, it represents a sizable innovation. It can also form the platform for a logical extension of the new relationship into actual joint ventures undertaken in concert by suppliers and their customers on the basis of genuine operating and profit-sharing partnerships.

THE SALES SUPPORT SERVICES SYSTEM

In his role as a consultant, the consultative salesman is the manager of a professional business service system. He manages the application of his own personal services, of course. But he often requires a greater diversity of services and a higher degree of expertise in each service category than he himself can hope to apply. Most of these services, although not necessarily all of them, can probably be supplied by the consultative salesman's company. Others will have to be made available to him from outside sources.

To enable its consultative salesmen to gain easy access to corporate services, top management will probably find it most efficient to systematize its sales support services as a business resource. Such a "3-S" system would include many of the services that are commonly available to back up a sales force in the field: technical services, customer application services, and some marketing services. But a truly comprehensive support system will go considerably beyond these typical offerings. Financial profit planning services will be a control resource for the consultative salesman to draw on, since it is a keystone function in the business planning process. Information center services will be almost as important. Vastly expanded marketing services may also be required, especially in the areas of sales strategy development, sales training, and marketing research.

By regarding each of its internal operating functions, both line and staff, as resources for the use of its consultative salesmen's clients, a supplier will be essentially opening its entire corporate resource capability to the benefit of its high-profit, heavy-buying customers. Department managers and staff service directors will be on call to the consultative salesman to apply their expertise to his customer's problems in addition to their normal duties on behalf of their own company operations. In effect, this will endow a supplier's top management with a dual responsibility similar in nature to that of the consultative salesman. They will be "line" in their internal operating capacities and "staff" in their external consultation services.

The consultative salesman will have to act as the manager of this corporate mix of personal services. His parent company's corporate resources will provide most of his talent mix. But he will also be able to contract with external, independent services to supplement his own corporate services or to provide him with expertise in specialty areas where the promise of unique accomplishment is required or where performance must be founded on a great depth of experience.

Each of the components in the consultative salesman's support services system must be of truly professional quality for the same reasons that the quality of the salesman's product line must be beyond reproach. In fact, the quality of the salesman's service mix may be even more important in determining whether a customer decides to do business with him. Thus all product manufacturers will be forced to think of themselves as, and act the role of, service suppliers for their consultative salesmen.

To insure the ability of the consultative salesman's company to provide the quality of support services at the levels of frequency that may be required of them, these services will have to be marketed in the same manner as all consultation services. This means that they will have to be costed and priced so that their investment is returned at an optimal profit. It will be the consultative salesman's job to create the single best service system for each of his customers that is in keeping with its needs and that will be preemptive enough in value to command a premium price.

THE SALES COLLEGE

Whether consultative salesmen are made or born is a moot question. But just as not all men are born salesmen, not all salesmen are born consultative salesmen. Nor can all salesmen be taught to practice the principles of consultation at a professional level. Yet instruction in consultative selling is the only reasonable method that a company can adopt to generate a continuing source of top-notch practitioners. The marketing of their services and the educational procedure to guarantee their production and training must go hand in hand.

The need for an on-line educational facility to teach consultative salesmen their functions will probably spur the development of the in-house "business university" concept among major companies. Under this concept, the random nature of most sales training will be superseded by the creation of a true university approach to the education of corporate personnel. A broad curriculum of courses will be offered to each employee-student. Both internal and external educators and programs will be used. Participation will be mandatory, not optional, and will be a precondition of employment, which will then take on a dual-track composition: Track 1 will be the position at which each manager must work. Track 2, to be traveled in parallel, will be the education that each manager must gain. Within the university, which will serve the entire corporation, there can be a sales college whose curriculum will be devoted to sales management. A major aspect of this curriculum will be the education of the consultative salesman.

Through a wide variety of educator-taught and self-taught programs, the consultative salesman will be educated at the home offices of his corporate university, at outside campuses and management education organizations, and through correspondence courses that will follow him wherever he may be. There will be no need for refresher courses, since learning will be continuing, not sporadic. All work will be graded and critiqued, and actual credits may be awarded at the degree level upon successful completion. To offset the considerable cost of the university's operations—and specifically those of the sales college, which may make up its largest student body—major companies can open enrollment to the consultative salesmen of other, noncompetitive organizations and thereby serve the needs of smaller businesses as well as convert at least some of their educational costs into income.

THE SALES COMPANY

A sales department composed of consultative salesmen is actually a consulting organization within the parent corporation. It is a simple organizational step to recognize this fact by spinning out the sales consultancy into a wholly owned subsidiary sales company whose services are retained on a contractual basis by the parent company.

Giving autonomy to the sales force by means of a quasi-independent company would professionalize its practitioners in a way that no other organizational act can equal. At once, sales takes on the symbolic form of expertise: a discreet talent package chartered to "do its own thing." Sales force morale can be bolstered by a new sense of identity, a new opportunity to achieve the titular and financial rewards of corporate rank, and the chance to add to normal forms of compensation by means of stock options that award equity in the enterprise, rather than merely salary and commission.

Another advantage accruing to the consultative salesman as a corporate practitioner is the fact that contractual relationships can be made with manufacturers and marketers who are not directly competitive with the parent company but utilize similar channels of distribution, depend on similar sales expertise, or can benefit from the synergistic effects of joint selling.

From the parent company's point of view, there can be important fiscal and service advantages from the spun-out sales company. Operating as an enterprise on its own, yet still benefiting from parent company control services and management counsel, a sales company can hope to act more in the manner of a true profit center than an internal sales department. It can control its fixed costs with greater precision and anticipate its variable costs more accurately on the basis of annually contracted service agreements with its parent and nonparent customers. And it can charge professional fees for its consultative services, over and above its income from sales.

As the market segmentation of a sales company's parent organization increases in sophistication, an original sales company spin-out may become segmented, too, into two or more specialized businesses. Each of these individual second generation sales companies will then be able to concentrate on its own market segment. To serve the needs of segmental concentration, sales companies will become more and more customized to the requirements of their markets. In its product and service systems, its methodology, its nomenclature, and even its geographical location—and certainly in the personality and experience characteristics of its consultative salesmen—each sales company will be an organization tailor-made for its customers.

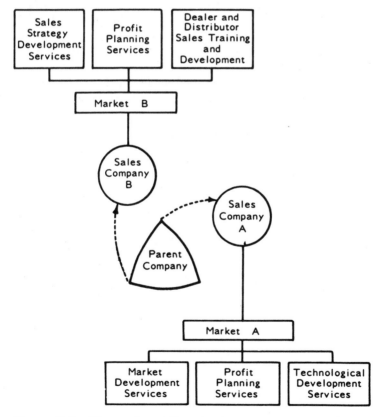

Figure 5.2   The custom-tailored sales company concept.

One form of evolution of the specialized sales companies created to serve specific market segments is shown in Figure 5.2. Here, the parent company has spun out two sales companies. Each company serves its own market segment, for which it is named and for whose needs it is custom-staffed. Its mix of services, and the policies by which they are applied, are both geared to its market's needs and are therefore likely to be highly individualized. This helps define the company as a business entity, endows it with a preemptive image, and gives it a firm grip on the acceptance of its market.

The sales company idea will provide a natural home base for the consultative salesman in residence with his customers. It will also be, in effect, a working alumni association of its parent company's sales college and probably the heaviest-buying client of its parent's sales support services. Through these interrelationships the sales company can tie together the total system of major innovations in the next generation of consultative sales management.

INDEX